A FAITH THAT WORKS

A FAITH THAT WORKS

DON LATHAM

Contents

Preface

In this book, I have set my Christian experience in the context of my career. After relationship with God and family, this is the most important area of our lives. It was tempting to include many other stories of wonderful events at conferences, church weekends and services, universities and colleges, ALPHA 'away days' and the like, but they can be told another time. The emphasis in this book is upon a faith that works, especially in that vital part of our life – our work.

As you will see, my progress over fifty years of Christian experience has not been easy – because of my frailty and mistakes, which God has turned around for good. With His help I have achieved my ambitions, and there is more to come. My hope is that, as you read the book, your faith will be stimulated, and that you will be challenged – and amused. This is the story of an ordinary person working in public service management. It is illustrated with true stories which will encourage you to let God fulfil the desires of your heart. As I look back on my life so far, I can identify the people who have influenced and inspired me, especially those who have built up my Christian faith. Understanding how faith works does not enable you to twist God's arm. It puts you in the place to receive what He has prepared for you.

Don Latham
September 2013

One

HOW IT ALL BEGAN

The Treasurer, Norman Marsh, was a small man with thick glasses. He sat on the arm of a brown leather chair in his impressive Victorian oak panelled office in Wolverhampton Town Hall. His deputy, Derrik Hender, was full of intense enthusiasm as he stared at me with his penetrating eyes. I answered their questions in a relaxed way, still not being sure what career I wanted to pursue. Those were the days of choice!

The informal interview had been arranged for me by one of my teachers who had an interest in local government, his wife being a prominent labour councillor. My latent ability at maths, he thought, could be put to good use in public service.

When offered a post as a trainee accountant, I had no idea that I was the first non-grammar school boy to be given the opportunity. What appeared then to be a casual, almost accidental, start to a career was later to be shown as God's plan for my life in one of the most important aspects of our existence – that of work.

The year 1956 proved to be a most significant time in my life. I was head boy at school and mad keen on sport – playing in most of the school teams and captaining a number of them. My greatest passion was athletics. Every day I was out on the road, running – often with my older brother David across the 'seven corn fields', the open countryside near our terraced home in Wolverhampton. David was a long distance cross-country runner and I was a sprinter. That year I was at my peak. I could run a hundred yards faster than any woman in the world. My problem was beating the men! One of the people I trained with at the brand new Aldersley Stadium became an Olympic champion.

It was all good fun and healthy competition. I enjoyed winning, and leading others, but the most important thing instilled in me at school was to do my best. When the opportunity came to stay on for a year, as part of a 'guinea pig' group to do 'O' levels, it was not a difficult decision to make. It was a good chance of another year of sport, to retain the victor laudorum, and to enjoy the benefits of a second year of being head boy!

My father had died the year before and, although his death had been expected, following a long, painful illness, it was still a shock for me. My brother had come to school and I was called to the Head's office to be given the news. Then there was the party after the funeral. I found it upsetting when people I had known for years, through the chapel we attended in Cleveland Street, seemed to me to behave as though life would simply go on. Of course it had to, yet it was different. From having been a home which was always full of people, where mother seemed to spend her life in the kitchen preparing food for a constant stream of visitors, it had become suddenly empty.

Chapel had been a way of life instilled in me by my parents and confirmed by attending an excellent infant and primary school, St Luke's, later made famous by a machete attack on the children and a brave act of protection by assistant Linda Potts. This was Church of England education at its best. The Reverend Bottomly came in to teach Religious Education every week. For some reason, at eleven years of age, we all found his name amusing, but he made the Bible come alive. Chapel attendance on Sundays was often three times during the day but, despite all this learning, I had never made a personal commitment to Jesus Christ – until that summer, following a tennis match against another church, St Jude's.

I was set up so innocently when asked to play, on what I had thought would simply be a social occasion. When the youth leader suggested an open-air meeting at the end of the match, my only option was to grin and bear it. At least we were in a village – Albrighton – and no-one would know me. I stood at the back of the group and thought of other things – the new football season, the girls in the group I hadn't noticed before.... The sounds were familiar to me and, as we stood, I gently swayed. This seemed to me to be a sign of spiritual maturity in our church on such occasions. You had to be careful not to sway so much that you fell over, otherwise that would have given the game away.

Swaying gently backwards and forwards, as I had seen my grandfather do when he stood to pray, and thinking of other things (like football!) I was amazed to find the youth leader's hand on my shoulder, indicating he wanted me to speak next. I must have swayed forward at the wrong moment. He took this as a sign of assent. I found myself facing the group and speaking of Jesus. I had heard it all before but now, in an instant, I was challenged, because I could see that the others in the group believed what I was saying. They evidently had a relationship with Jesus which I knew nothing about – and they were smiling and nodding approval. It was a shock. I could hardly wait until the next Sunday, when I made my own commitment at the end of the service. The preacher was a regular, and he was using a repeat sermon. When you are bored, and usually sit on the back row, you almost count the words to keep sane. My brother had escaped this boring routine by National Service, and I had thought this would also be my means of escape.

The thing I am most grateful for is that I was taught how to become a Christian. It is a personal recognition that Jesus is the Son of God, that he died for our sins and was raised from the dead; that we need to repent (turn around) from sin and to ask his forgiveness, welcoming him into our lives and begin to follow him as a disciple. This I did in the early autumn of 1956, sitting in the back row of a chapel which I had attended throughout my childhood years.

I have had many exciting and amazing experiences, a number of which appear in this book, but this is without question the most important. There were neither flashing lights nor a voice from heaven, but I knew it had happened. 'Trust and obey, for there's no other way, to be happy in Jesus, but to trust and obey', is what the congregation was singing as I came up from under the water at my baptism a few months later. My Sunday school teachers were crying, my mother was crying – and I was pleased to have made my public confession of faith.

At school, together with another pupil, Jim Gough, we started a Christian Fellowship, with the enthusiastic support of our music teacher, Miss Blandford – who was a Methodist lay preacher. I became Chairman and we took school assemblies. The Christian Fellowship grew rapidly. It had a remarkable impact on the culture of the school, the behaviour of the pupils and academic performance. All this, together with my five GCE 'O' levels, provided the foundation for an accounting career in Local Government.

How I admired Derrik Hender, who went on to become Chief Executive of the West Midlands. He said, 'Latham, it will be a struggle, but you will qualify.' I made up for intellectual inadequacy by sheer hard work – and I did struggle. His words, I know, were meant to motivate, but actually fed into my insecurity and lack of self-confidence. The lecturers at Wolverhampton College of Advanced Technology did all they could to inspire, teach and train positively. The best was Louis Ballam, a small man who wore a white coat to avoid getting chalk on his suit, and who taught accountancy with such enthusiasm that you felt disappointed whenever you failed to meet his expectations.

When you look back on your career, you see key choices, decisions, people whom God has used to motivate, inspire and drive you on to greater things. One such person was Tom Rees. He was a well known Bible teacher and evangelist at that time. Each year, a large group of us would travel by train to Hilldenborough Hall, an impressive hotel on the seafront at Frinton-on-Sea, for a houseparty with a strong emphasis on tennis, using the immaculate courts of the East of England Lawn Tennis Club. Tom would address us with great eloquence and authority each morning. It was here that many life-long friendships were formed, and Christian standards of morality and ethics were established as a foundation in our lives. It was also great fun, which was enhanced when the venue moved from the green sward and beach cricket of Frinton to mountain walks in Switzerland, especially in the beautiful resort of Wengen in the Bernese Oberland. Tom Rees was a man of stature in every way. He could recite whole books of the Bible which he had committed to memory, and he believed in excellence. Everything he did was well planned, expertly organised, and of a high quality – and I was determined to emulate him.

One of our enjoyable activities was singing. Four of us – Derek, David, Reg and myself – sang barber shop quartet style and we were much in demand around the declining chapels of East Shropshire. We had great times – and our first experience of preaching. I like to think that we did not cause the decline. At least we reduced the average age of the congregation, and we always enjoyed good hospitality.

Life in the Town Hall was challenging and pleasant; making tea with the other office juniors, getting the political buzz of a balanced council, with members brought in from hospital for crucial debates and decisions; counting at elections and seeing, first-hand, democracy at work. Auditing, accountancy, costing and technical work followed each other in a time of rapidly gaining experience. It was competitive, and I wanted to give my best, but the end result was long hours of work and study. I had no father to turn to, but God gave me other men to be my mentors and role models. Men like Jack Stordy, who had built up a highly successful business and who sought excellence in all he did, whilst adopting Christian ethical standards of honesty and integrity; and Derrik Hender, who would call you to his office and ask challenging questions, with the purpose of training for the cut and thrust of professional work in a political and public environment.

Over these early years, the foundations of my career were being established. Friends were leaving home for college, university and new jobs. My best friend, Derek, died a week before his twenty-second birthday. I remember being given the news at hospital, with his mother, that he only had a few days to live, and the tears that were shed on my shoulder as we travelled home on the upper deck of a municipal trolley bus. In his illness he had been inspirational, and it built in me the desire to live life to the full, and in a way that would influence others for good.

I had itchy feet, and was finding accountancy examinations a great test and extremely hard work. All the circumstances around me made me unsettled and ready for a move. Friends in London would invite me for a weekend in their exciting basement flat in Bayswater. To me, this was not the centre of life they made it out to be. I opted to respond to an advertisement for a trainee post in Devon, where I could continue to study in style. Devon for me was a damp version of heaven, and I drove down to Exeter in my Austin Sprite, full of expectation, if not a little apprehensive about the prospect of leaving home.

The interview went well. I thought the Personnel Officer, who asked most of the questions, was the Treasurer. Notwithstanding the fact I got this wrong, and that the man sitting nonchalantly in County casuals, Ossie Saunders, was the real man I had to impress, I was offered a post which would enable me to get new experience and to complete my training. A month later I drove down theA38, my belongings packed all around me in my pale blue 'frog eye' Austin Sprite, with those mixed emotions you feel when starting anything new.

Two

THE FIRST MOVE

The accommodation which had been recommended to me was not easy to find, so I booked in for a couple of nights at a guest house – the Elizabethan, in Magdalen Road. First impressions of Exeter on the Saturday were not good. I discovered later that I had chosen the least impressive part of the city for my first walkabout. Sunday morning brought about a complete change. I turned up at Belmont Chapel, to find a thriving church who were ready to give a wonderful welcome to a Christian bachelor. The hospitality was tremendous and, from that first morning, the diary was filled with lunch engagements stretching weeks ahead. Dr. Charles and Nora Simms were my first hosts.

County Hall was an imposing new building on a large estate. I was really looking forward to the challenge of a new job. One of my motivations for making a move had been my desire to have a change from being an auditor. I had done a twelve month stint in audit and the time seemed right.

'We have changed our minds and are putting you into audit,' the Treasurer said, as he welcomed me to Devon County Council. The disappointment was soon dispelled by the experience of four days a week driving round the county on audits, and spending Friday in the office writing reports and preparing for the next week. The place not to commit a fraud in Devon was on the coast. We were always there auditing, and my diary looked like a West Country tourist guide!

A new Chief Auditor came, and one of his credentials for leadership was to beat all the previous best travel times to audit destinations. Happily for me, I mainly travelled with Joe Frost who was nearing retirement. For him, life – and driving – was at a leisurely Devon pace. My greatest danger was falling asleep as his passenger, especially as we drove back to the office on those dark winter evenings. The office was full of exceptionally talented people. Not surprisingly, Devon attracted able people and retained many who would have been Chief Officers in other local authorities, but who stayed because of the quality of life they enjoyed with their families. This was an attitude I found hard to accept at that stage but later, looking back, I now see the wisdom of it. I could so easily have made the same decision, especially as the guest house offered me good terms to stay on a permanent basis – which I gladly accepted.

Belmont Chapel consumed all the spare time I had when not studying for accountancy examinations. From junior work, teaching a group of 10/11 year olds on Sunday, I progressed to be one of the youth leaders for the most thriving youth club in Exeter. It was an activity-based and action packed organisation, led by an inspirational young man called Bernard Partridge. The annual highlight of the programme was a weekend houseparty. With Alan Pavey and 'Bung' Taylor, I was to form a song and dance act which performed on these special occasions. All of this was to prove excellent experience for my later career! Seriously, this was not only great fun, but a time when we saw the lives of many young people transformed by a personal encounter with Jesus Christ.

The balance between work, study and Belmont was not always easy to maintain, but life in Devon was certainly full and exciting.

The invitation, from one of the older church members, to a table tennis evening was something I thought I should fit into my social diary. Having completed my three course meal with coffee at the Elizabethan, I duly turned up at eight o'clock – to find I faced another three-course meal and coffee prior to the table tennis. Mrs Alford was a renowned cook and, as the bachelor, I had to be well fed – I was not expected to turn down the second helpings. By nine-thirty, the last thing I felt like was table tennis. I confided my predicament to the person next to me at dinner and it all seemed highly amusing. This would prove to be the significant beginning of a friendship with a woman who, unknown to me at the time, would become my mother-in-law.

At the office we had the shock of one of the accountancy assistants dying in his sleep – not at the office, but in bed at home.

He was replaced by an auditor who, within six months, was off work with stress and a severe nervous condition.

'We would like you to have a go, Latham,' said Malcolm Thompson, the Deputy County Treasurer. So I moved from audit to accountancy, the major part of the job being to look after the capital accounts of the authority. Confidence is that feeling you have before you understand the problem – and I was full of it. Providentially, at all stages of my career, people whom I respected trained me and set a wonderful example. Alf Haywood was a brilliant Chief Accountant with a great sense of humour. If things went wrong, his favourite saying was, 'The whole matter has been very badly handled.' With him sitting opposite me, I learned both the discipline of work organisation, and that demanding work could also be fun.

I was about to become party to a West Country arranged marriage. Actually it was arranged by God, ably assisted by my mother-in-law. We both knew we were being set up to meet each other, and Hilary was as determined as I was that nothing would come of it. As she came into the room, I knew she was the right person for me. The next day, we went out on our first date – a drive down the south coast, with the hood down and the sun shining. Hilary was a student at Bedford College, London University, so we only saw each other a couple of times before the Easter Houseparty, but I had no doubts and planned a proposal during the trip to Switzerland. This was the first time the youth club had ventured abroad – and we were unprepared for the snow we would find on the Jungfrau. Down in the valley at Wilderswil it was all bright green and with the first signs of spring flowers, but once we got up the mountain, on went the skis and our uninsured party disappeared in all directions on the nursery slopes. It was good that one of our party was an experienced skier, and with much shouting and prayer we all survived.

I had found a bridge over the river and planned this as the spot for the big question. The night was pitch black as we walked out, leaving a high-spirited group in the chalet. We got to the bridge and I looked into Hilary's face – or at least the general direction I thought she was standing – and there was silence. What I expected to say next was that there would never be anyone else, I would wait for a lifetime; what mattered most was her happiness. In fact

17

the standard speech that all men rehearse, but to my amazement she said, 'There is nothing I would rather do.'

Long engagements are not recommended, but we had to wait for Hilary to finish her degree. Although we planned for a new house on the edge of Exeter, it seemed right to make a career move to avoid buying and selling a property – and more likely to avoid letting ambition die in beautiful Devon.

A job was advertised in Wiltshire, and I thought Salisbury would be good for a couple of years. It was a surprise to me to find that Trowbridge was the county town. The surprise turned to consternation as I walked round the town on a damp autumn day in 1965, prior to the interview. It was consternation because I knew I was going to get the job! County Hall was an imposing building, and the fact it was in Bythesea Road, when we were miles from the coast, only added to the sense of unreality.

I sat in the waiting room with four or five other candidates in their blue suits. They were biting their fingernails. I thought, 'Haven't they seen Trowbridge?' How could I get out of this with honour? I had applied because Ray Moon, the Treasurer, was on the CIPFA (Chartered Institute of Public Finance and Accountancy) Council. This was going to be good for my CV and I could not turn it down. A great idea came to mind: give a relaxed interview. One of these other intense candidates was bound to get it.

It was about midday when I faced the interview panel, chaired by Sir Henry Langton. He was the epitome of a county gentleman, and was a race horse owner. I was 'laid back' – and they absolutely loved it. When offered the job, my only thought was, 'How do I explain this to Hilary?'

In this simple story I was later to learn a most important principle: the power of words to be creative or destructive. Some time before, when attending a lecture in Bath, I had walked alongside the river and said, 'Father, this is the place I would love to live and serve you.' Trowbridge, like any other place you visit, was on the edge of the map. Over the page, Bath was only ten miles away. Within two years, God had worked it out and shown us a new house in the countryside, which was an easy drive to work, and from which we could centre our life in Bath, the Heritage City of Europe.

Living on my own for a few months was not easy. A new

garden had to be created. This kept me busy and produced pains in my body which I thought were terminal – apparently a common occurrence of pre-marital tension in men. My only concern in St Leonard's in Exeter, on a typical August bank holiday when it sheeted down with rain, was that Hilary would walk more quickly down the aisle, so I could get the contract signed and settled. This was the second most important decision of my life, and one I have never regretted.

We would not have guessed that a two-year career move would lead to almost fifty years of life in Bath and West Wiltshire, and that I would progress from junior accountant to Chief Executive. I was to learn the lesson of taking things one step at a time. God has a plan for our lives that covers our mistakes, but he usually only shows the next step.

Three

ANGLICAN EXHAUSTION

I was settling into work at County Hall – now, at last, a fully qualified accountant. It was less demanding and interesting than Devon and I wondered about the wisdom of the move. Hilary had obtained a teaching post at Bath Technical College and was having to work extremely hard in preparation. In the months on my own, I had looked without success for a church that would match the dynamism of Belmont Chapel in Exeter. When some neighbours invited us for tea, suggesting we went to church with them in Bath, we gladly accepted.

Walcot (St. Swithin's) is an inspiring Georgian church. Its parish includes the well-known Royal Crescent and the Circus, and the Snow Hill council estate at the other end. What first impressed me was the size and age of the congregation. The church was full, and there were many young people. The Reverend Gordon Jones, the Rector, shook hands on the way out – asking who we were. A good-looking man, with swept back silver hair and beaming smile, he was a truly dynamic preacher, with a great sense of humour.

We were surprised that the unexpected caller at our house on Monday evening should have been the same man. A former businessman, he came straight to the point. 'We have been praying for someone to lead our youth work,' he said, 'and I believe you are the answer to our prayer.' It would be easy if God's guidance were always so simple and clear. We went to meet the other youth leaders, and were introduced in a dirty crypt, which there were plans to renovate and adapt for the youth fellowship. We quickly became involved in a demanding and exciting work, with a membership that built up to two hundred, most of the young people also coming to church on Sundays.

The football team brought in the boys, and the boys brought in the girls! Our programme was vigorous and activity-based, and addressed the social and spiritual needs of the group. In respect of the latter, we were not making progress with the football team. Guest speakers giving an epilogue at the club would be howled down for every sentence which had a double meaning. We got so desperate, we prayed about the situation – and the week's houseparty in Wales brought about change beyond our wildest dreams. Dr Ashton spoke in simple but clear terms of the challenge of a life committed to following Christ – and the boys responded. There was no emotional pressure; they had seen the truth.

At County Hall, I was getting so frustrated I volunteered for a move into Audit. Another lesson I was to learn is that God does not want us in a rut. We may have to wait for the next thing to be prepared, but God wants us to use and develop our talents and abilities. He is also the God of wisdom, who will give it to us generously if we ask. I was to play a major part in a feasibility study. It would change significantly the procurement methods of the council, with substantial financial savings and benefits to the community. Supporting the Supplies Officer we argued the case and won, despite some having other views about the new ideas. I gave lectures and provided consultancy advice to the private sector on how to sell into the public sector, particularly local government.

Success gets you noticed. Within a year my role was developed to undertake technical work for the Treasurer, and this was so successful that within another year the job became purely technical, and I developed a close working relationship with the Treasurer, Ray Moon. He had the habit of calling me into his room late in the afternoon for a chat, just to share his latest ideas. It was very stimulating but he rarely asked me to sit down. It was at least a good preparation for charismatic Christianity where the prerequisite, above all others, is to have strong legs. Our conversation would go on to approximately six thirty, and there would be the sound of a car horn – his wife having come to pick him up. He would say goodnight, and quickly excuse himself. But he was one of my many mentors; a gentleman, but firm, who was both professional and dedicated to the highest standards of public service.

The momentum was maintained. I became a group accountant within another year. This meant managing a team of accountants providing financial support for a number of the council's major services. These included children's, welfare, and health, which would become part of a new Social Services Department. My colleagues thought I was crazy applying for the post of Assistant Director of Social Services (Management and Administration). Over one hundred and fifty applied – mostly graduates – and my five 'O' levels won the day. This was another lesson. Five promotions in six years. If God gives you favour, it can happen. Our part is to honour Him by giving our best and doing our work to please Him. If you seek to excel in your work, to give your best, to be creative, and are open to new ways of working and you are enthusiastic, it tends to lead to promotion – providing personal satisfaction and challenge.

Hilary had found teaching progressively easier. She was now ready to break her career to start a family. So Peter, and two years later Victoria, were born. Life was full. I was always busy, trying to balance the pressures of work with family and church commitments. We had handed over the thriving youth work to others and I started to serve on the Parochial Church Council. Deanery Synod, Diocesan Synod, Missionary Committee, Churchwardenship all followed. The church was truly evangelistic and we embarked, with some success, on activity after activity to make the Good News known to people.

The parish weekend was perhaps the single most important event of the year for church members. We were to have our first introduction to Brunel Manor Christian Centre in the autumn of 1968. Arriving a little late, we saw that the gothic-style building looked rather run down. The following morning, we were impressed by the magnificent setting, with panoramic views over Torbay. Little did I realise that I would later become a Trustee, and play a small part in the transformation to a high quality Christian holiday and conference centre. Since that time, I have returned to speak at many conferences and church weekends.

I was suffering from Anglican exhaustion, though I was barely aware of this at the time. Only a change of Rector spared me from such hectic schedule. I was not the only member of the congregation suffering from the effects of a frenetic lifestyle to have taken advantage of the interregnum to relinquish some church activity. It was essential to get life into a better balance.

My job in Social Services was extremely challenging. The budget was about £20 million and we had three thousand staff. It was vital to have the right Chief Administrator to work with me, as I urgently needed help to set up the new department. Because of the pressure it was tempting to appoint following the first advertisement, but the wise County Personnel Officer would not let me do so. He proved to be absolutely correct. We advertised again and Joe Holder was so evidently the right person. If you rush and panic into a decision it is rarely appropriate. The old adage certainly applies to appointments, 'If in doubt, don't.' Joe became a tower of strength for me and I was to learn so much from him about people management, and having the moral courage to deal with the real issues of under-performance. He also showed me how positively to motivate and lead people to give their best and to develop their talents to the full.

Together we tried to change the world in a year! I was only spared the effects of stress by going on a ten-week management course which was in itself intended to be very stressful. In fact it proved to be light relief, compared to the work I had been doing. It made a major impact on me, and on my approach to management. Professor Stewart, of the Institute of Local Government Studies at Birmingham University, was the visionary academic whose dynamism ensured that we returned after our fortnightly weekend break, and remained for the last lecture on Friday afternoon. It was the content and his sheer enthusiasm for the role of local government, that he never lost, which ensured one hundred per cent attention. The course was unquestionably competitive, but I learned things about strategy, leadership, motivation and delegation which enabled me to be much more effective on my return to Wiltshire.

Nevertheless, a personal experience outside the office was about to result in a more radical change to my way of doing things than anything a ten-week management course could achieve. I was now to face up to the reality of my life, and see what I was really achieving.

Four

FROM PRESSURE TO POWER

One of the things that kept us all going, during these hectic years, was the church house group. We met on Tuesday evenings in our home, and developed strong friendships with the twelve to fifteen regulars who came to study the Bible and pray about the practical issues we all faced. The new Rector, PhilipMyatt, talked more about the person of the Holy Spirit than his predecessor had – not that I took too much notice. With hindsight, I can see that the group was somehow different – also that Hilary was different, and that she had conversations with our Christian student lodger from which I felt a bit excluded.

'The church is organising a weekend sponsored by the Fountain Trust,' Hilary said, 'and I think we should go.' I had heard rumours about this Trust. It was something to do with the Holy Spirit, and causing problems. So I definitely didn't want to go. I was a good Christian – and listened to rumour. I make the important decisions at home ... so we both turned up on Saturday morning. To my surprise, the teaching was practical and helpful. The afternoon sessions were entitled, 'Baptism in the Spirit and Healing'. Hilary wanted to go, and I definitely did not, so I offered to look after the children. These things were not for today, but only for the time of the Acts of the Apostles. I volunteered for what was safe... a time of worship in Bath Abbey.

Despite all my church activity – or perhaps because of it – my spiritual life was dry. I rarely prayed, and only read my Bible to prepare for a group, or teaching session. Yet I was a brilliant actor and played the role of enthusiastic Christian leader. I actually thought that you can't be too disturbed in the Abbey. Having preached in the Abbey a few months previously, I had not disturbed anyone. The lesson I was about to learn is that God does not want us to find security in a rut. God is most interested in our personal development and our relationship with Him. He has much to teach us, not least that we come to the point of really trusting Him.

Much to my surprise, as I pushed the door open, I saw that the Abbey was full. As I walked down the aisle to find a seat, I noted that there were many people I knew. They nodded to me. I nodded back. I now think that any sign of life in church is encouraging. This was to be my first experience of a charismatic style of service. The congregation sang the songs through not just once, but often three or four times. After half an hour I had worked out the system. They seemed to move on to the next song when I had joined in – so I quickly joined in. People had hands in the air when they sang, which I had never seen before during my eighteen years of hyperactive Christianity. There was a pause. In the silence someone prayed in a language I thought was Japanese. 'How wonderful that one of our visitors (we get so many in Bath) should feel free to be able to pray in their own language,' I thought. A moment later someone spoke out something in English. I can't remember exactly what was said, but I do remember the thought that God put into my mind.

'You have had a relationship with me since you were fifteen, but you lost your fellowship with me years ago.'

This thought was so strong that it was difficult to concentrate on the preacher – and back at home again I explained to Hilary what had happened. For me a bombshell dropped, because Hilary responded by saying that she had been trying to tell me for months that she had been to see Philip, the Rector, who had prayed for her. She had been Baptised in the Spirit and now spoke in a new language that she had never learned (the gift of tongues). Worst of all she was happy about it. Any normal man would have said, 'That's very nice, dear,' and carried on living a normal life. But, because of my particular Christian background, I felt so angry that God had done this, I could not watch Match of the Day. When I went to bed, I could not sleep.

Walking round the lanes of Limpley Stoke on a clear starlit night, I was in confusion. My scientific wife, my best friend, had had an experience you cannot have today. I vented my anger by erecting a wooden 'Wendy house' for the children, which had just been delivered. The job was done before breakfast. My plan was to go to church and after the service lambaste the Rector with my sound theology, then kill him. It all worked out, until I faced him in the vestry and was so exhausted after a sleepless night, erecting the Wendy house and surviving the family service, that I heard myself say, 'Philip, I have to know the power of the Spirit.' We shed some tears, and I went to the Rectory after lunch, and he prayed.

What did I experience? A great sense of peace, and a desire to read the Bible. The next day I went out and bought a new copy; this was theology made easy. Yes, I did want to speak in tongues, because I found it difficult to learn languages when I tried. To be given one without trying would be a miracle. It was in trying so hard that I became utterly frustrated, and it was made worse by the Rector praying with Hilary in their Holy Spirit languages, when I could not. When it did happen, it was coupled with an amazing experience, which was worth waiting for. One Saturday evening we went to St Philip and St Jacob's (known as Pip 'n' Jay) in Bristol, where the Reverend Malcolm Widdecombe did a remarkable work over many years. As I walked past the bookstall at the back of the church, I noticed a booklet which seemed ideal. It was something like Praying in Tongues Made Easy – just what I needed! The booklet was paid for and slipped into my pocket.

On Sunday morning I read the booklet. It was all so easy, it seemed. You needed to co-operate with the Holy Spirit, make a noise with your tongue and lips, having asked Jesus to baptise you with the Spirit. After lunch I lay on Peter's bed with the bedroom door closed and carried out the instructions. To my astonishment, my stumbling noises turned into a fluent language. At the same time, a brightness came into the bedroom, which was so wonderful to experience that I thought, 'If I open my eyes they will be burnt out of their sockets.'

It was so special that I did not try it again for a week. The following Sunday I walked down to our Norman church in the village, and asked God if I could do it again. This time there was no bright light, but the experience was to have a dynamic effect on my life and work over the following years. The Christian's work is part of his worship to God. We were created to work, and the first priority is to do a good job. Working in Social Services was a challenge and joy because colleagues were so committed to help others improve their quality of life. There was no conflict between good management and good social services.

The power of the Holy Spirit was given at Pentecost, both to equip the disciples as witnesses and to replace their fears with boldness. The first sign that new things had happened was when one of the Christian doctors in our practice rang me to see if I could help with a patient - one of my staff, off work with a stress-related illness. We prayed that, if this was right, there would be a clear indication from God. The next day, my Chief Administrative Officer, Joe Holder, who dealt with personnel matters, asked me if there was any way I could help. I rang the colleague, who lived in a neighbouring village, asking whether she would like a chat, inviting her home at a time Hilary would also be there. Taking an afternoon's holiday, we met, and I first talked to her as a good manager would - which left me feeling depressed. I then asked her permission to tell her my experience of knowing Jesus, sending her off with a copy of St. John's Gospel, and a book called The Happiest People on Earth. She read them, and asked to come back. It was the next Monday when she became a Christian. We prayed for her to be filled with God's Holy Spirit, and to be healed. She rang back three days later, describing herself as 'a new person'. She was back at the office the next Monday.

Another colleague had had serious surgery and, when we met in the lift one day, it was quite natural for me to ask how he was. He described pains in his body, and a ringing noise in his head, from the time he woke up to the time he went to sleep. I felt immediate compassion and, instantly, a thought came into my mind,

'Pray for him; I want him to be healed.'

'You don't pray for people in lifts,' was my next thought.

'He is a subordinate of mine. What if nothing happens?' By the time I had listened to these doubts we had reached the third floor and gone our separate ways.

'I blew that Father, bring him to my office if you want me to pray for him,' I said, sitting at my desk. A few moments later there was a knock on my door. I had no doubt who was standing the other side. He came in and, after we had briefly discussed some matter of finance, I said to him, 'I believe God wants me to pray for you, and you are going to be healed.'

'Please pray,' he said. I went round my desk, gently laying

hands on his shoulders and, not knowing how to pray in English, prayed in tongues. It all seemed natural – not least to my secretary, who sat in the next room and could see what was happening, because the door was open. She went on typing, as though we did this every day!

A few months later, this colleague told me that, from the day we prayed, the noise, which I was to discover was called tinnitus (and was incurable), had diminished day by day, until it went completely. More importantly, through the intervention of another Christian colleague, he had made his own personal commitment.

Praying for healing was not a ministry I had sought, but it came about through two experiences. The first was attending a healing service in a United Reformed Church in Bradford on-Avon, when the speaker was Ian Andrews, another accountant. I sat on the back row with a pain in my right side, the result of a kidney infection, although I did not realise it at the time. I was incredulous as people went forward for prayer and fell gently backwards. A few moments later, they got up – apparently healed. I thought, 'There is no way I would go forward unless the next thing he says is, "there is a man on the back row with a pain in his right side."' Ian had been gently walking to and fro, listening for words of knowledge from God. The next thing he said was, 'There is a man on the back row with a pain in his right side.' I was trapped, and weakly went forward for prayer. The pain left me and I was healed. The only problem was that it came back the next morning.

A friend at church said to me how good it was that I had been healed, and I told him it had come back. 'Rebuke it in the name of Jesus,' he said. 'You have been healed.' I did, and I was.

Fred and Vera Tobin were older members of our church, and they had seen their son receive a miraculous healing of his left leg. They had arranged a house meeting, to hear a young American Pastor, Larry Huggins, who was visiting the city. I went to encourage them, only to find I was the only one there. It was to be an exceptional evening for me, as I could ask so many questions of a man who had a personal relationship with God, in a way I had not seen before. He prayed for me, and I received God's anointing to pray for others. This was an evening when my life changed.

Alongside this, work in Social Services was challenging and rewarding. We brought about major changes and service improvements. Meetings of the Directorate were held in the smoke-filled room of George Newton, the Director. One his favourite sayings was, 'The good can be the enemy of the best.' We were determined to aim for the best. I enjoyed working in the political arena, and arguing for resources. Other departments emulated the management and financial practices we had introduced. We put into practice devolved management – long before others even started to talk about it. We adopted a zero-based approach to the budget, introducing performance measurement to improve the quality of service we were giving to some of the most vulnerable people in the community.

Those were the days of growth and long-term planning. I produced the first, and the last, ten-year plan for Social Services. This was part of a joint planning process with the Health Service. The Chairman of the Health Authority, Sir Maurice Dorman, a former Governor of Malta, described it as one of the best documents he had read. My English master from school, who had encouraged me into Local Government, would have been amazed!

It was time to move on, but the longer we had stayed in Wiltshire the more I feared making a move. Success can obscure the fact that one is in a rut. I was settling for less than God's best.

Five

LEARNING FROM MISTAKES

'Coo', (our nickname for Hilary's grandmother), had gone round a roundabout the wrong way in her Mercedes. To the shocked man who wound down his window to speak to her (this was before the days of electric windows and so-called road rage) she responded, 'Haven't you ever made a mistake?' This became a popular family saying. I was to learn that God can use our mistakes, big or small, to develop our understanding of Him and to prepare us for the future.

Re-visiting the Isles of Scilly, one of our regular favourite holiday destinations, I realised that I felt stirred up about past events in my life, without understanding why. The Director of Social Services was terminally ill, and life had suddenly become unsettled. A book by an American Baptist minister was to explain part of what I was experiencing. He explained how, after he had been baptised with the Spirit, things from his past had come to the surface. God had shown him that what was happening was that He was clearing all the rubbish out of the 'pond'. That really helped me.

Walking round Hell Bay on Bryher, I thanked God for all He had done in our lives. I heard myself hand everything over to God, including my career and ambition. He had been waiting for this, and I felt an immediate release of a burden. Walking round the next bay, I was singing in the Spirit. It was a very special time.

Hilary and the children were having an extra week on the Scillies, so I returned home on my own. In the pile of post was a letter from Birmingham. I had been called for interview for the post of Assistant Chief Executive of the West Midlands. In order to satisfy my desire to advance my career, but without really wanting to move, I had salved my conscience by putting in occasional applications for posts. My first reaction was one of excitement but, within three days, I was in total confusion. Having given my career to God, was this a test – that I had to show I really meant it? Or, having given it to God, was He now giving it back to me? The essential lesson I was about to learn was that, 'a double-minded man can receive nothing from the Lord.' To confuse the issue, the Director had died, and many staff were suggesting that they wanted me to be appointed.

By the time I set off for Birmingham I was in turmoil, and determined to give up the chance – unless God gave me clear direction to go ahead. The first night was the usual social occasion, when you prove to a group of councillors that you can converse easily and eat food properly. On the Birmingham New Road, the dual carriageway from Wolverhampton, I stopped at one of the many sets of traffic lights. A bearded old man in a brown coat bent down. He looked into the window of my blue MGB GT and asked for a lift into the city. Thinking this could delay me, I shook my head and accelerated away as the lights turned to green. It was only later that I remembered how, on glancing back in my mirror, I could see no-one standing there.

The meal went well, and the conversation was easy. The next day there was the main set-piece interview in the morning, to sort out a short list: forty-five minutes of questions from a politically balanced panel. From the first question, answers flowed easily. It was evident to me, as I left the room, that it had been very well received. How simple is God's guidance, and yet I could not see it. When things go so well it is obvious that the way has been prepared for you but, because of my confusion, I walked away before the final round of interviews and the wonderful possibility of working for the man who had first appointed me, and who was one of the people I most admired in local government.

Driving home, I knew I had allowed myself to be cheated out of a God-given opportunity. Friends back in Bradford-on-Avon told me that on the Friday they had asked God to send an angel to give me direction. It was exactly at the time I refused the man a lift into Birmingham.

Subsequently, the Director of Social Services post was given to a more experienced colleague. This was the first time I had failed an interview in Wiltshire. The experience left me feeling shattered and depressed. Over the next three months, two further opportunities arose and the same scenario applied: a new job, followed immediately by another which appeared to be more interesting and, having not taken the first opportunity, the second failed to materialise.

We face tests and trials in this life. If we do not pass the test first time, God is so good; He gives us opportunities to take the test again. These were difficult, tough times. If God tells you to move on, the most secure thing to do is move. The old job was quite different, working for a new Director. It became much more circumscribed, so I felt as though I was in a trap of my own making. Instead of waiting for God to show me the way ahead, I helped Him by suggesting a plan to return to the Treasurer's Department as Assistant County Treasurer. It was not a job I really desired, but it would provide a change, security, and an opportunity to advance my career.

It was an interesting experience, writing my own job out of the organisation as part of a management restructuring, then waiting for agreement for the move, which enabled a colleague with a heart condition to take early retirement. Such experiences revealed how little I really knew God – and showed how much I had yet to learn before I could truly trust Him.

The move took place, and I advised the Council on financial matters concerning Highways, Planning, Environment and Performance Review. I was responsible for Exchequer services – about a hundred and thirty staff – and all professional training. It was not very exciting, but what kept me going was reading the Bible before the start of each working day. I started to read it through twice a year, as well as studying it.

All the Christian committees on which I served, I thought, could not survive without me. But God clearly told me to give them all up. Our Archdeacon friend, Reg Bazire, could not understand how I could survive without the stimulation of Diocesan Synod. Sometimes God requires us to let go of things before He can do a new work. The new things He was about to ask me to do were not what I wanted to do, but were to prove most exciting and rewarding.

Another Christian friend, David Brayton, invited me to go to a dinner with him at the Royal Lancaster Hotel in London, hosted by the Full Gospel Businessmen's Fellowship International. That was on September 19th 1977. The founder, Demos Shakarian, was to attend. It was amazing to see a large dining room full of five hundred and forty businessmen, wearing their city pinstriped suits, praising God and then listening to a few men telling their personal testimonies. I discovered that some men had underwritten the evening by £4,000, and the previous week only seventy-nine had booked. This memorable evening was followed a few weeks later by an early morning drive to Manchester for breakfast. David was keen to see whether there would be interest in opening a chapter (the name given to a local FGBMFI group) in Bath. I was not as enthusiastic, but was swept along by him. He booked the Pump Room, confidently expecting two hundred. I agreed, but only had faith to book for fifty coffees. Two hundred came. Despite a rather poor quality video, and many guests going without coffee, there was a very positive response to the suggestion of forming a Chapter. Some weeks later, a group of about twenty men met at Fortts Restaurant, with the National Directors, Alan Jones and Bob Spilman. To my astonishment, I was selected as President.

During the previous weeks, Hilary had been getting a verse coming into her mind from Acts. 'Do not fear, but speak and do not keep silent; for I am with you... for I have many men in this city.' When hands were laid on me for this new task, a word of prophecy flowed from Alan, which included the words, 'Do not fear but speak out, for I have many men in the city, and I have given you the keys of the city.' It was like electricity going through me when I heard those words.

Meetings at Fortts restaurant in Milsom Street were very exciting. We were to see many make a commitment to Christ, including colleagues I invited from work, at dinners and breakfasts in the relaxed and natural environment of a good restaurant.

I had often invited a senior colleague in Social Services. In the end he chose to come, when a simple but powerful testimony was given by Graham Dacre of Norwich, the proprietor of a quality car dealership. It was wonderful to see him standing, with four other men, making his personal commitment public at the end of the evening. The next morning, he could not wait to tell me what had happened.

'When hands were put on my shoulders I felt power flowing through my body and had a vision of Jesus standing behind me. Back in my seat, I saw that a man with severe hearing loss was now able to hear, and I knew what it was like when Jesus walked on the earth.'

Clive was Deputy Director of Parks for Bath City Council. After coming home from work that evening, his car refused to start again – so we went to fetch him. At the end of the evening, as he came to thank us for the invitation, I had a clear thought for him.

'You are going on a course and you will know that God has provided the place for you.' I did not know that he had applied to go on a Masters degree course at Loughborough University, where two hundred people had applied for the twenty places. A few days after our dinner, God spoke to him very clearly and directly as he read St John's Gospel, Chapter 5, verses 24 – 25, and he committed his life to Christ. A few weeks later, having heard nothing after an interview at Loughborough, he phoned the Director of the course, to be told that he did not actually have the qualifications required. However, that very day, the Director was writing a letter to the University Senate, asking them in Clive's case to waive the requirements and invite him on to the course! That simple word of knowledge was confirmed, and Clive's commitment to Christ was to have dramatic effects on the life of his family and career.

These were good times. We organised monthly praise and teaching meetings at the Pavilion, attracting between seven hundred and a thousand people. Many of the well-known Bible teachers came to these meetings, uniting the Christians in the city. George Carey, who had just become Bishop of Bath and Wells, was one of the speakers who made a great impact. What I had not expected was that, in a short time, I would be travelling all over the UK and Europe, undertaking speaking engagements.

That was one God-given opportunity. The second proved to be Youth for Christ. Our curate asked me to be Chairman of a newly-formed group for the city. I had done years of youth work and had no desire to go back to it. So I said politely that I would think about it. He was persistent, so I said I would pray about it – and then felt I had to pray, to avoid feeling guilty. You should never try to box God in, but I did, by saying, 'If you make it clear by Saturday, I will do it.' Hilary had been getting the verse from Isaiah, 'Behold, I am doing a new thing' consistently coming to mind. We thought it was a word of encouragement for a friend we had been counselling. On the Saturday morning I jokingly said to Hilary, as the postman came down the drive, 'Here is the confirmation about Youth For Christ.' Amongst the letters was a brown envelope franked BYFC. Opening it I drew out the printed page which had in bold letters, yellow on black 'Behold, I am doing a new thing.' I immediately telephoned through my acceptance of the Chairmanship.

There were problems to sort out and the task I faced was not easy. The lesson to be learned was that one should only act on a word from God. If I have failed to do that, any action taken subsequently invariably proves to be wrong and leads to regrets. We surmounted the problems, aided by the wisdom of the Reverend Clive Calver who, at that time, had overall responsibility for BYFC. We appointed our full-time worker, feeling that it was right to do so, despite our having no money! Each month we prayed and, often on the last day, we received a gift to cover the costs of his salary. Many of the young people on that committee have continued doing an important Christian work.

These new areas of opportunity had emerged following a mistake. God knew I would make the mistake, but He knew that I would learn through the process of restoration in my work. It was five years later that God spoke to me afresh, as I talked to Hilary in the kitchen. The Lord said to me, 'After seven years I will restore you.' This linked up with the passage in 2 Kings 8:1–7, in which the mother of the boy restored to life by Elisha is given back everything, following seven years of famine. Only two years to go! They proved to be action packed.

At work, I had ideas about how to increase the efficiency of council services. God gave me wisdom, particularly in my role as one of the officers advising the Staffing Sub-Committee. One day, I was due in Halifax to speak at a dinner. This committee was considering a very delicate disciplinary matter that involved a very senior and high profile member of staff. As discussion continued, the committee seemed no nearer reaching a solution, so I prayed for an answer, not least so I could get away. It was as though a letter was dictated to me; it came so clearly into my mind. Being the only non Chief Officer in the room, I hesitantly asked the Chairman if I might make a suggestion – and dictated the letter back. It was warmly received and it was to resolve a potentially fraught complex personal problem. I was learning the lesson that God is interested in our work every day, and will give us wisdom when we ask.

When invited by the Chief Executive to meet the new Chaplain to County Hall, I was impressed but when, a few weeks later, I came late to a lunch-time informal meeting to hear Ron being told by a social work colleague, who was a very new Christian, how to live with pressure and stress, I suggested that we pray. We did, and he experienced such peace that he did not move from the chair for some time! He received God's healing and a fresh anointing for parish ministry, and for an effective counselling and pastoral ministry to the large number of staff in County Hall.

One lunch-time, through the visit of Isabel Chapman, a woman with a remarkable story, we were to see about twenty staff make a commitment to Christ. I did not have courage to invite two of my close colleagues, for whom I had been praying – but they both came to the meeting, and made a positive response.

God wants us to have fulfilling work to do. One day I was speaking at a Baptist Church in Chippenham, on the Christian response to issues of unemployment and work. In my work you have to be non-political, so it was with some consternation that I saw a councillor coming down the aisle at the end of my talk. This was to be the start of a friendship, confirmed the following week by a visit to my office. We were in the middle of a conversation and I felt a pain in my back, thinking immediately, 'Oh, no! Please don't make me pray for an employer.' Praying for a colleague was one thing, but not an employer. I made a bargain with God, that I would pray for her if she asked, confident that she would not ask the Assistant County Treasurer for prayer. She next said to me, 'Oh, Don, I have sciatica so badly I have to hang on the doors at home to relieve the pain – and I have just pulled a door off its hinges. Would you pray for me?' I duly went round the desk and prayed. Within a moment she moved her back, and the pain had gone. A few weeks later, a Christian doctor prayed with her at a meeting where she made her own personal commitment to Christ. She subsequently became Chairman of the Social Services Committee, following a surprising political change. She often used to come for prayer for wisdom in chairing the Committee.

Waiting times, I had to learn, are not wasted, but are times of preparation. Seven years does not seem long if it is in someone else's lifetime! But in your own it is a long time. I began to count the days....

Six

HOW TO GET MORE FAITH

Details of European Fellowships for short study tours were circulating round the Social Services Department. We were having to consider ways of determining priorities for the provision of services. Demand was outstripping available resources and I thought this would be a useful study, providing fresh impetus in my job. Applying for Holland, rather than my preference, Sweden, which I thought would be oversubscribed, I sent off an application. I was restricted to these two countries, because they were prepared to accept applicants who only spoke English. I was accepted for Sweden, primarily to be based in Stockholm.

A couple of weeks before the trip, we attended a meeting in Bradford-on-Avon where Hilary's eye was caught by the book entitled *Anointed for Burial*. It was about a young couple who had gone out to Cambodia, from a Church in Stockholm, and had witnessed a revival and many miracles. Having read the book, I was determined to find this church on my first Sunday in Stockholm. It was a momentous visit. The city was absolutely beautiful and, on my first Sunday, I sought directions but nonetheless arrived at the wrong church! This church building seated five thousand people, and had the largest choir and orchestra I had ever seen in a church. It was wonderful – but not the right place. The local authorities and health institutions were really welcoming. Every day was spent researching. However, I seemed to know more about the issues than they did, and related my ideas to top professional staff and academics. They gave me a 'Golden key to Stockholm', which meant I could see all the public sights and buildings without charge – so my schedule was full. Eventually, I found the church

I had sought. It met in a converted theatre seating one thousand. The first night it was closed, but I could hear the music group practising. The next night it was open and packed to capacity. I had to sit on the back row of the balcony, the view obscured in part by a pillar, but made acceptable by a television screen.

The first time I understood what was going on was when the young speaker started to speak in English. His name was Benny Hinn. When he had finished, amazing things started to happen all over the church, as people were spontaneously healed and filled with the Spirit. Not understanding Swedish, I did not understand the notices, nor that he was to be there the next night, and for the weekend. But I turned up just in case. Arriving much earlier, I still had to sit in the balcony. It was again astonishing to see the things that happened. At one point he called for someone in the balcony to come forward for prayer. There was no movement. He then described the person and said, 'I am going to ask God to tell me your name.' He called out a name, but there was no response.

'I am going to ask God to tell me your age.' There was a clatter as a seat went up, and a woman fitting the description moved rapidly down the aisle. She did not reach the front of the church, but fell and lay there under the power of the Spirit. I was so impressed, not least by his leaving the platform during the time of people receiving from God, as if to ensure he received no personal glory for what God was doing. I remember thinking how wise this was, avoiding the danger of pride. God told me to expect to see similar things happening in England. In some measure I have, often to my surprise, as we will now see.

It was great to know the power of the Holy Spirit in a new way. But I felt a concern. It was fine to know I had inside me the same power that had raised Jesus from the dead. But how could I cause that power to have an impact for good upon others? Where could I go to receive teaching about this? Did I have to go to college? This would be impossible, given my family responsibilities. In any case, I knew that my primary calling was to serve God at my place of work.

The answer came in a surprising way. A young American couple came to run a highly concentrated course, only a few miles from where we lived. When I heard about it, I signed up. There were only a few of us, but Gale and Bob Buse, fresh from Rhema

Bible College in USA, were so inspired and anointed that every evening with them felt like two gourmet meals! Some of the things they taught were not new to me, because I had been well taught previously. These truths seemed, nevertheless, to move from being 'head knowledge' into my spirit. It is easy to say we become joint heirs with Christ – but it is quite a different thing really to believe and know it; to understand how faith operates, and the difference between faith and hope; to understand what it means spiritually to be a new creation, made righteous. Added to this, there is the matter of understanding the importance of confession, the power of words and the name of Jesus; learning how to be led by the Spirit, and how to receive God's wisdom; how to pray; how to receive and move in gifts of the Spirit; and praying for healing; most importantly, learning how to walk in God's love.

It was a life-transforming course. Within a couple of weeks I was preaching at our church family service at St Andrew's. A good friend, who ran a highly successful car dealership, came to me at the end of the service.

'Where have you been?' Julian asked, as he recognised the immediate impact the teaching had made on me. This course, and the study of the Bible that followed, prepared the foundation for what I was to teach and put into practice every day. As we learnt new things, I asked God to give me personal illustrations and experiences, which would help me in turn to teach others.

One of the signs that you have the Spirit of God in you is that you wince every time you hear someone blaspheme the name of Jesus. I am getting so old that I remember the times when at a Wolves match at Molineux you heard little bad language. As a young boy, it felt quite safe in a crowd of fifty thousand at a derby game against West Bromwich. A man would never swear in front of a woman. Now we have the language of the gutter on the terraces and, even worse, in our homes, through the medium of television. Blasphemy has become routine in modem Western culture.

Sitting at the office one day, I asked God to give me an illustration of the power in the name of Jesus. At that moment, a junior member of staff from the cashier's office brought in some cheques for me to sign. I had personally to sign cheques for over £40,000 in the Treasurer's name. I love spending other people's money! The cheques were signed 'A.F.Gould' and the junior left my room. God said that there was my example. In the Treasurer's absence, I had the delegated power of attorney, to use the legal phrase, to sign cheques on behalf of the Treasurer – in his name. The bank would honour the cheques, as though he had signed them himself.

All the power has been placed in that name which is above all names. From that time, when I prayed for people, I asked God to show me how Jesus would pray, then prayed in His name, with amazing results.

A sign that we are sons and daughters of God is that our lives are guided and directed by the Holy Spirit. The Rector telephoned me one morning, saying he wished to talk to me about a church matter, at lunchtime if it were possible. I looked at my diary and said that if I could return from visiting a computer centre in Bristol, I would see him. Having cleared the morning post with my secretary, I drove over to Bristol and called at a petrol station, both for petrol and to ask the way. These were the halcyon days when people served you. Having had the tank filled, I asked for directions to the centre. The attendant looked as though he wasn't certain where Bristol was, so I thanked him and prayed for God's direction. Praying quietly in the Spirit, it was as if by putting thoughts in my mind that God said, 'Left, straight on, left, next right, straight on'... and so on. After about three miles the thought came, 'Pull over.' I did, again enquiring as to the way.

'You have stopped opposite it,' the young man on the pavement said – and I had. Having travelled to speak in so many places, this is a method I have had to resort to on many occasions when my hosts have not sent directions.

Tony was a male nurse in a local hospital. A Christian friend, Catherine Kirby, had through her lifestyle and her ability to answer his questions, led him to a point of committing his life to Christ. He came to our house for prayer, and we prayed that he would be Baptised in the Spirit. He was a new Christian, with no prior understanding of the Christian faith, and he simply received, in a way we have now seen thousands receive. That night he prayed in the new prayer language God gave him. The gifts of the Spirit do not require spiritual maturity, but just a simple faith to receive.

That was Thursday. Three days later, Tony said, as we left church, 'God has told me there is somewhere you need to be on Thursday, and that I am to come to look after the children.' I wanted to hear an American speaker who was coming to Bristol that night, and knew Hilary should be with me, but she had to go to a lecture. As it happened, the lecture was cancelled. We arrived at the hotel for the meeting. I thought we would sit at the back and see what happened. At the end of the evening, Larry Huggins, who was a last minute replacement for the advertised speaker, was having words of encouragement for people. Looking up, he said, 'Don, please come forward; God has a word for you.' Then, after a brief pause, he said, 'Hilary, you need to be here as well.' We stood there together and out flowed a word in rhyme, indicating things for our future and, in particular, that we would minister together. We were ordained together for ministry – unlike many friends who had gone into the Anglican ministry, not in a Cathedral, but in the back room of a hotel. And the whole arrangement had been confirmed by a Christian only a few days old in his faith!

The invitations to speak came in increasing numbers and great variety. Locally, speaking on behalf of the Bishop as part of his team dealing with the financial needs of the Diocese, provided many opportunities. Our willingness to give provides real evidence of the level of our commitment and trust in God. Again, I looked for practical evidence of the truth I was teaching. I want a faith that works – and one of the clearest areas where God will speak to you is about giving. On a number of occasions we have given exactly what people have been praying for. The most dramatic happened one Sunday morning during the family service. The thought came to make a gift to friends, who were involved in Christian work in the city. I asked, 'How much?' The thought came straight into my mind. It was so accurate, in pounds and pence. The thought was immediately followed by doubts and questions. 'This is your crazy idea.' 'It's too much.' 'It's too little,' and so on. For me, this was confirmation that the first amount was correct. After lunch, I suggested to Hilary that we pay them a visit, having written out a cheque for the strange amount.

We were warmly welcomed, and invited to stay for tea. I slipped the cheque onto the mantelpiece as we left. A few days later we had a letter, explaining that they had no cash to meet an outstanding gas red demand note and they had prayed that if they were still in the place God wanted them to be, He would confirm it by meeting their financial need. As you have guessed, the cheque was for the right amount.

God says He will give back to us in the measure we give to Him. God's Word is the manufacturer's handbook for a faith that works. This is not a faith that can manipulate God, but it puts us in a place to receive what He has prepared for us – even a hundred-fold on what we give. That was the teaching God said He would prove to me. I had not asked for it, but God said He would. I forgot about it, until twenty-two months later when I was driving to work through the country lanes. The thought came to me, 'It's done.'

'What's done?'

'The hundred fold return on what you gave.'

A few weeks later, I discovered that someone had given us a gift in a building society account. It was a hundred times what had been given that Sunday. I often say that if I were not British, I could get excited!

Seven

ACTION LEARNING

The telephone rang in the middle of the night. It was an invitation to speak at a men's weekend in Missouri. I immediately said 'Yes', thinking they must have made a mistake. The next morning I thought it must have been a dream. Yet, a few days later, the formal invitation letter arrived. I travelled with a Scot, and another local government officer from Cheshire. The flight was uneventful, and gave us time to get to know each other. Our journey by car, down from St Louis to the camp by the Lake of Ozarks, was at a leisurely 55 m.p.h. Although they appeared from the outside to be very basic, the log cabins proved to be both well equipped and extremely comfortable. The lake we overlooked seemed larger than the English Lake District. It was good to see men of all shapes and sizes, and all types of occupations, mixing together – including many fathers and sons. I have never travelled so far to say so little, but it was a new experience, and we were made very welcome. On the Saturday night, the main speaker was overcome with laughter at one point. This quickly spread to everyone in the building. It was quite an astonishing scene. I was only thankful that people at home could not see me being part of such an event.

The other two men had exciting itineraries planned for them at the end of the weekend, but nothing appeared to have been arranged for me – other than hotel accommodation near St. Louis. Apparently by chance, at the last minute, an invitation came to attend a house meeting and to have supper. Shortly afterwards, someone invited me to what seemed a very lively church but, as I was by now committed, I had to decline. Driving back, we used a CB radio to call ahead. The weather had been quite turbulent all weekend. I discovered we would be making a detour, if necessary, to avoid tornadoes.

At the house group, there was a short study from a passage of the book of Revelation, which I was not asked to lead. What was I doing here? Why did I stay on? Shouldn't I be back at home with Hilary and the children? The study finished, and we went into the kitchen for a buffet supper. At the end of the meal, a young couple to whom I was talking asked me to pray for them. So, not for the first time, I had to apologise to God and felt thankful He had led me to be there.

We went into the lounge, to find the rest of the group in prayer. This was not in itself unusual, apart from the fact that one girl lay prostrate on the floor praying. I did what any self respecting Englishman would do, that is I sat as far from her as I could!

Any sense of embarrassment quickly departed, because there was a wonderful sense of peace and God's presence. After a time, she looked up and said, 'God has told me to pray for you.' They gathered round the chair. Together, she and her husband laid hands on me and prayed. It was at that moment I knew I had received what had been prepared by God for me on this trip to America. During coffee, I told them of how a few years ago, a young American pastor had come to Bath, and that he had prayed for me with such an impact. They asked his name. When I told them they became very excited.

'He was our Associate Pastor in Tulsa, Oklahoma. We have only just moved to St Louis. You are not Don and Hilary are you?'

'I am half,' I replied.

'He told us about you and we have been praying for you by name every day since,' they said. God had brought us together in a house in St Louis.

It was with great expectancy that I went to speak at a meeting arranged in a Catholic seminary in a small town the next day. It was a town struck by a tornado. It was awesome to see fully grown trees that had been sucked out from the ground. Telegraph poles were snapped off like matchsticks, and a trailer home was twisted like a corkscrew as the wind had gone in one end and out of the other.

'I have put a greater power in you than the power of a tornado,' was my thought. 'A tornado creates destruction and fear. The power I have put in you heals and brings peace.'

At the end of the time of teaching, I invited people for prayer, and the first was Baptised in the Spirit. She burst into song.

'Not a spectacular voice,' I thought. At this point it seemed as though everyone came forward for prayer. I was to discover later that the lady who had sung was well loved and known in the local community. She had been born with a speech impediment, which had been healed when we prayed!

Coming home with this new anointing, I began to receive invitations to give talks in Europe,which then led on to the Caribbean, and return visits to the USA. God used FGBMFI, first in Bath and then in a rapid way, when I became a Director of the Fellowship responsible for the South West, speaking at breakfasts and dinners throughout the UK. It was a programme of action-learning, which God had prepared for me. I became used to late night or early morning driving and sleeping in many spare bedrooms – or children's rooms, where youngsters had been moved out for the guest speaker.

I never turned down opportunities to speak, though at times I regretted this, as on the occasion of a visit to Newtown Chapter in mid-Wales. It was a wet night, and I had chosen the middle route through the countryside of twisting roads and beautiful scenery. It was not my policy ever to arrive early, but to be on time – because I preferred not to be briefed about any guests. The travelling time was spent concentrating on the road and praying in the Spirit. There were about one hundred people at the dinner and, as usual, there was a testimony given by a local person before I was invited to speak. The majority of guests seemed to have come from one church and, as I started to speak, I began to feel that my journey might have been wasted – not being aware of what God had planned. At the end of my talk, I moved round to the front of the top table, asking if anyone wanted prayer – with no great expectation that anybody would respond. A lady stood, and walked one or two paces towards me. I heard myself speak with such an authority, 'You have had a spirit of infirmity for eighteen years. In the name of Christ, be healed.' She crumpled, and lay peacefully on the hotel carpet. It was then that a flood of people began coming forward for ministry.

The lady had experienced several disabilities following a railway accident, and had continued to have painful spasms. She later wrote to me:

'Praise the Lord that He healed me and I have since had no recurrence of the trouble that has caused so much suffering through the years. It is like taking a new lease of life at seventy. I don't know how to thank the Lord; it is so wonderful.'

Another woman came forward for prayer, and I was told that her non-Christian boyfriend intended to hit me as he saw me pray with her. He could not move out of his seat. More importantly, as a result of this experience, he subsequently made his own commitment to Christ.

Annual FGBMFI conventions were held in Blackpool, at the Norbreck Castle Hotel. At my first convention I heard such great men as Steve Lightle and Charles Colson. Never did I dream that my time would come to speak to one thousand people in this annual venue – especially when the main speaker was Kenneth Copeland. During one afternoon session I was listening to Kenneth speak on faith. I had a problem – not with his teaching, but the fact that the conference committee asked me to speak that evening. I felt obliged to agree because they said that, having prayed about it, they were sure I was God's choice. I thought, 'How can I follow this great man without looking foolish?' When I confided in my friends, they agreed that I couldn't! It is at times like this that you pray with special urgency, when you are desperate!

Some friends from Warminster came to see me at the end of the afternoon session, and asked if I would go with them to pray for a friend, Jean, who lived in Blackpool. They had brought her to the meeting, but she could not stay for prayer as she was in so much pain. Reluctantly, I agreed. They drove me along the sunlit Blackpool promenade, my eyes captivated by the varied shades of concrete, and highly coloured bulbs. Only one thought came into my mind, over and over again. 'I want Jean to know Jesus.... I want Jean to know Jesus.... I want Jean to know Jesus.' This was to be a lesson in God's priorities.

We arrived at the row of neat, terraced houses, which reminded me of my own former home in Wolverhampton. After a short delay, Jean made her way to the door to let us in. She was crippled with osteoarthritis. There were four of us, plus Jean, in the small, immaculate room. Keith, a big man, stood and I sat alongside Jean, on the settee.

'Jean, God has spoken to me. He wants you to know Jesus.'

'I would love to,' she said, 'but something stops me.'

'Can I pray for what stops you? There is a prayer which is so effective at dealing with unbelief – it even works in theological college,' I said.

'Please pray for me,' she replied. As soon as I prayed, she gasped and fell back on the settee. Now, looking straight ahead, she kept on repeating the name 'Jesus'. At this point, Keith fell flat on his face on the floor, missing a perfect collection of bone china by inches. Now I had a problem because, as she repeated the name of Jesus, she squeezed my fingers – and they were becoming white. The moment Jean had received Jesus, she was healed! She came to the convention that night, and walked in front of everyone, without her walking sticks. One of her daughters came that same night and made a commitment. Jean's husband was an atheist; an atheist who had real difficulties when he got home from work that day and found his wife was no longer crippled, and talking about Jesus. He only survived a few weeks before he too responded to the love of Jesus. Twelve months later, arriving late for the start of the convention, we were put on a table with Jean's family and one of the Christian doctors from our practice. That evening he led the thirteenth, and final, member of Jean's family to the Lord. Salvation had come to a whole family in twelve months, and it had started with Jean's healing. She told me later that when I had prayed for her she had a vision of Jesus standing in front of her.

Speaking in Europe at 'Advances' (FGBMFI is a totally positive organisation and does not have retreats), and at conventions, also provided training times for me. God's demonstration of His powerful presence often compensated for my inability to speak other languages. After a few days teaching on the Swiss/French border, I was taken to stay with a young couple who were to take me to my plane the next day. I had flown to Mulhouse, rather than Strasbourg, because the flight was cheaper. We went to buy food at a huge supermarket, and later sat enjoying a meal together, when the telephone rang. I did not understand much of the conversation, other than that they were declining an opportunity to be on a Christian radio programme the next day, which happened to be

Easter Sunday. They confirmed this is what they had done – because it was early in the morning. Jokingly, having done some radio work, I said I would do it for them. This produced an instant response. The producer was telephoned and I was 'volunteered'. My host would act as my interpreter.

We arrived at the studio at 6.45 a.m., in time for the programme which was to start at 7.00 a.m. Sitting in the studio, with headphones on, I smiled to the producer sitting behind his glass screen. I asked my interpreter, 'When is my two or three minutes in the programme?' He looked bemused.

'You have an hour, from seven o'clock,' he said. This was time for instant prayer; it was only a few minutes to seven. The only thought that came to mind during the opening hymn was, 'Get him to interview you.' He nodded at the suggestion, and it ran well, until another hymn was used. 'You will now have a message for the audience,' my interpreter said.

'I will now have a message for the audience – please tell me what it is?' What I said, I do not remember. I know it flowed easily, and was being well received by the producer in his glass box. It was now fast approaching the end of the programme. The thought came that I should pray with the audience that, on this Easter Sunday morning, they would acknowledge Jesus as the resurrected Son of God, seek his forgiveness, and welcome him into their lives as Saviour and Lord. It was like an afterthought when I said, 'There is someone at home with a deadness in the right side of the face, and you are deaf in the right ear; if you will put your hand on your face now, you will be healed.' We sang the final hymn. The clock hands came round to exactly 8.00 a.m. This was to teach me that God wills not only that we should be ready to respond to His prompting spontaneously, but also that when we trust in the guiding of His Holy Spirit, He orders events perfectly.

At home, we were enjoying Easter breakfast when there was a call from their pastor asking if I would speak at church that morning. Arriving at church, we observed much excitement. The pastor was explaining that a woman had telephoned the studio at the end of the programme. There was a regular audience of about eighty thousand, in this largely Catholic area of Europe. She was a Baptist and, near the start of my talk, God had spoken to her to say that I would say something specifically for her. So she had listened intently to this English local government accountant. Just before the end of the programme, the Holy Spirit had said to her, 'It is what he says next.' Then I had said, 'There is someone at home with a deadness in the right side of the face, and you are deaf in the right ear.' She had had neuralgia for some months, resulting in a deadness in the right side of her face. She also had lost her hearing in her right ear. When her hand was placed on her face, in response to the 'word' I gave, she felt a warmth flow through her. She was healed, and her hearing was restored.

A men's camp in the autumn was to bring another challenge. Arriving at Vienna airport, I wondered what had happened. No-one had come to meet me. My hosts had been delayed by holiday traffic, arriving just as I was planning a weekend of sightseeing. We drove through magnificent scenery to our hotel, high up in the mountains. One of the things this trip taught me was always to go well prepared. They told me after supper that they had decided I was to do ten teaching seminars over the two and a half days. It was wonderful to see more than thirty men with their Bibles, ready and waiting to absorb the truth of God's Word. Most of them were from a Catholic background. At the end of the second evening teaching session, one man came forward. God gave me a word of encouragement (prophecy) for him. The other men applauded, then formed a queue. They all wanted a word from God. I seemed to be on my feet for hours as, one by one, God gave me a word for each man. One of them, a scientist, had volunteered to entertain me for the night. On arriving at his home, I was introduced to his wife.

'Don had a wonderful word for me in the mountains. After supper, I will get him to repeat it for you,' he said.

Where did he come in the queue? As we sat together after supper I called on God's help. The tears in his eyes confirmed that I was able to repeat, word for word, what God had given me before.

Why could we not see in the UK miracles similar to those which happen in other parts of the world? 'Why could we not see the blind receive their sight?' This was a question I had put to God. I prayed and fasted for greater understanding, and a release of all the gifts of the Holy Spirit which the apostle Paul said we should desire. Then something special happened at an FGBMFI dinner at the Cafe Royal, on 11th February 1987. This was the Fellowship at its best: a good meal, a musical item – then I was on to speak.

At the end, I invited people to receive Jesus, and a number did so. Then I invited people to come forward for prayer. They did not form a line, but came up in large numbers. After a few minutes during which many were being prayed for, a woman became a bit excitable. Observing that a number of guests were heading for the exit, I decided to intervene. I expected to tell her to be silent, firmly but quietly, in the name of Jesus. Standing in front of her, I was surprised when I said, 'What can you see?'And she replied, 'You are beautiful.' It was a dimly lit room. Nevertheless, for those who know me, you will appreciate that it was a memorable moment.

Mali, a Jewish woman, had come to the meeting with inoperable blindness in one eye. I asked her to explain what had happened. After my testimony, Mali was crying. 'I could see everything I had done wrong and I was sobbing.' When I asked those who wanted to receive Jesus into their lives to come forward Mali leapt to her feet and came forward with her friend Jane. She asked Jesus to forgive her for the past – for all the things that she had seen pass before her. 'I was just being lifted,' Mali said, 'God was lifting me as you lift a child.' She felt tremendous relief that she was forgiven, as if all her wrongs over the years had dropped away. And before she and Jane had returned to their seats, Mali experienced another miracle. Mali turned her head to look around and suddenly she shouted, 'I can see, I can see!' Her right eye, the one that had been too damaged for human hands to mend, was healed – working as perfectly as the left one!

We love to travel and, as you delight yourself in the Lord, He does indeed give you the desire of your heart. When a friend, Julian Scaramanga, phoned me to say God had told him that we were to go to America, I knew it was right – especially as God had told him to pay for me! Because he was paying, he naturally had the choice of seat on the plane, and chose to sit next to the window. I had the middle of the three – the one where you have no arms. It is always interesting to see who sits next to you on a plane, and I was to have a lesson that God orders the seating plans of jumbo jets. As we settled down for the journey, a lady came to sit next to me. I can safely use that non politically correct term because she was wearing a fur coat, and was also dripping in jewellery. As she rested her arms on the seat rests, her fingers drooped over the end because of the sheer weight of gold, diamonds and sparkling stones. I knew she was American – not because of the jewellery or the accent, but simply because she spoke to me, from the moment she sat down. I love American women, because they enjoy talking. This one enjoyed it so much that I could not get a word in. It was all about life in Los Angeles, and it seemed too good to be true. In the morning it was shopping or tennis. In the afternoon the jacuzzi, and the evenings were spent dining out at some smart, sophisticated restaurant. It was difficult to contain the envy. All this happened as we waited for our take-off slot, and trundled down the approach way to join the short queue. As we started our take-off, she paused for breath. I spoke my first words. 'Why are you so unhappy?' Julian would have climbed out of the window, had it been safe to do so. This is not a recommended opening comment to a stranger but, probably as a result of her nervousness about flying it released the floodgates. I was told about her unhappy marriage, family problems etc., etc., and, as always, my answer is Jesus. I told her, simply, how much Jesus loved her and, before we had reached our cruising height of 36,000 ft, she had committed her life to Him, her face running with tears and mascara. Part way across the Atlantic, I felt a pain in my body. This is often the way the Lord gives me 'words of knowledge' for someone's healing. I thought, 'Oh, no. We are on a jumbo jet and I am British. I can't go round the plane with a placard saying, 'If you want healing come to the front of economy class.' Nor could I ask the crew to make an announcement.

'Tell me who it is, Father,' was the simple prayer. My new sister from Los Angeles said, 'Don, I have had such pain from an ulcer. I can't wait to get back home.' Offering to pray, I rested my hand on her fur and prayed simply and quietly. The pain left her immediately. It was a joy to receive a card a few weeks later, confirming her new faith and the healing she had received in mid-Atlantic.

The training session at FGBMFI headquarters was very rewarding. I love the positive attitude that you find in America. Problems are just opportunities to be successful. Visions are big, and nothing is impossible. God wants the best for us, and from us, in all that we do. I was enthusiastic to see the work in Bath take off. I prayed for an increase in membership. My target was sixty and we were to see this achieved. We were believing to see a hundred men a year, as a minimum, to come into a personal faith in Christ – and we were to see this achieved.

My mind was buzzing as we boarded the plane for our return flight. 'Bet you couldn't do that again,' I thought as I waited to see who would sit next to me this time. A girl in her late teens sat next to me and she looked English, so I just nodded and said, 'Hello.' As I looked at the string bag she put on the floor, I noticed a black book. Was it a Filofax? Or could it be a Bible? We were through our first meal, and I thought it would be a good time for a read. So I got out my Bible. This will guarantee either the start of a conversation or, alternatively, that your personal space will not be invaded. There was a wide-eyed reaction and a fairly obvious question about my being a Christian. It became evident through the ensuing conversation that here was someone who had experienced the Baptism of the Holy Spirit, only to be discouraged by other Christians from using the gifts of the Holy Spirit, especially tongues. I was able to show her the truth of the matter through the Bible. She was refilled with the Spirit as we enjoyed Christian fellowship over the Atlantic. This was simple 'action learning'. If I spent time praying in the Spirit, God would continually put me alongside people who were in need, or who were simply ready to meet Him through His Son Jesus.

It was through sharing everyday experiences like this that invitations came to speak at many churches. One weekend, for Christ Church, Winchester, was typical. The Reverend James Mitchell Innes invited me to talk to his church leaders on the Saturday, and to take morning and evening services on the Sunday. It was the weekend of the great storms of 1987, when the trees of Southern England came down, as did the stock market. For those who could hear me, despite the noise of hail on the roof, what I had to say seemed to be positively received. So I decided we would close the Saturday teaching with a time of prayer. I had already prayed for a number of people when an older man, Clarence, came to me saying he wanted to pray for me, which he then did. I then said to him, 'Have you got any problems?' He smiled knowingly, and told me of his major heart problems and the array of medicines he was taking, 'Let's see what the Holy Spirit can do,' I said, putting a hand on him and praying for his healing. After a few moments, he fell gently backwards and was lying on the carpet. Onlookers saw the colour flooding back into his cheeks, as he lay there. It was obvious, from his smile, that something was happening. The Sunday morning family service finished at about midday. By the time we had prayed for those who stayed behind for ministry it was half past one, and time for lunch.

The evening service was quite normal until the Rector asked Clarence to speak about what had happened the day before. He declared he had been healed, and this much-loved member of the congregation was silenced by applause – in an Anglican church! He had experienced a number of heart attacks and, following major heart surgery, had been virtually housebound, taking ten tablets a day. But now he said that he was healed. Given that testimony, it was not surprising that most of the congregation came forward for prayer at the end of the service – another late but glorious night. The story was reported on the front page of the church newspaper under the heading, 'Clarence surprises his doctors.' They had declared him, 'disgustingly fit'. Clarence said, 'The Lord healed me, and now He is using me to heal others.'

This was a pattern I was to experience in churches of all denominations, as God supplied opportunities for action learning. I wanted a faith that worked. The key was to seek God's anointing. That mattered more than anything. As the young pastor Larry Huggins had said to me, 'God makes room for the anointing.' In other words, God will create the opportunities. It was true that in the most natural, apparently unplanned, events, opportunities arose and we saw miracles – the greatest always being people turning to Christ.

Barbados provides a further example. I was speaking in a church about the power of words to bring blessing or curses. The Vicar realised then why he had had ME for two years. To escape the pressure of ministry in a large new housing estate, he had foolishly said, 'I wouldn't mind having ME for a fortnight, to have a break!' We prayed that night. He woke up in the morning healed. If I am under pressure, and need a break, I always say, 'I wouldn't mind a fortnight in Barbados' – and we went! Not knowing the local churches, I looked up the FGBMFI telephone number in the Barbados telephone directory.

'I want an all singing, dancing, clapping, good teaching church for Sunday.'

'We go to a Pentecostal church like that,' the person said.

'When do you meet?' I enquired.

'We meet at 7.00 a.m., 9.00 a.m., 11.00 a.m., 5.00p.m., and 7.00 p.m.,' he said.

'Why do you meet so often?' was my next question.

'Because the church building only holds a thousand.' We opted for the five o'clock because, I thought, they have to let you out by seven o'clock to get the next congregation in – and we could get back to our hotel for dinner which, at Sandy Lane, was quite special. They insist on your wearing a jacket and tie which, in an increasingly casual world, is a delight. We were caught in a downpour, which was like white water rafting in a Mini-Moke. Sitting in the church, dripping wet and gently steaming, we saw the huge building fill up with a smartly dressed congregation. There was not a pair of jeans to be seen anywhere. The Pastor sang us through the service, and the American university professor who spoke was so powerful that I can still remember his message today. There are not many preachers of whom I could say the same.

The person who answered the phone, Bert Topping, rang me back a few days later. Their speaker, for a breakfast at the Hilton Hotel, was unable to get there. They had prayed about the problem and wanted me to stand in as the substitute. I asked permission, and Hilary agreed that I could do it! So, on the Saturday morning, after breakfast at Sandy Lane, I went to the Hilton. The breakfast had attracted about sixty businessmen and, after an excellent short testimony from a young business man called Ward Simpson, I was introduced and spoke. In the time of ministry at the end, God gave me a very specific word for one of the men. I did not then know he was the Assistant Commissioner of Police, nor that the men had prayed with him before I arrived. The word was, 'Mr Griffith, you will have your man shortly.'

Early on the Monday morning, I was sitting on the terrace looking out at the sparkling sea and clear blue sky. The newspapers were delivered. Looking at the *Barbados Advocate* I was thrilled to read the headline: 'Assistant Commissioner of Police: "Our prayers were answered".' He explained that, at the prayer breakfast, he had asked for prayer for God's protection for himself and his men, and for assistance in recapturing a highly dangerous criminal. I had given him a word at the breakfast, and within twenty-four hours the dangerous criminal had been recaptured, without injury to the police. He said to the reporter, 'Contrary to what people may say, we know that we cannot do everything ourselves. The first person to put in front is God.' He added that his team gives God thanks for all things, '..As without God, nothing can be done.' Perhaps it was not surprising that we were invited back the next year to speak at the Caribbean Convention of FGBMFI and I was invited to speak at the church which has five congregations of a thousand each Sunday!

None of these things seemed to have been planned, and yet they were – by God. As you learn to take each step, and grasp every God-given opportunity, it is amazing how one thing leads to another in a way you could never have imagined, including growth of the most wonderful friendships. God has an action learning programme for each one of us. All we need to do is get into this plan.

Eight

GOD'S RESTORATION

It did not happen, and yet I expected God's timing to be perfect. It should have happened in August, but it didn't. I could not understand why there was a delay, so I kept on with a busy programme of speaking engagements. Over ten years, I did more than a thousand speaking engagements, most often in small meetings, but sometimes to a thousand and with radio and television opportunities to many more thousands. I have now prayed with over five thousand people to make a first time personal commitment – something which seemed impossible before that afternoon when the Reverend Philip Myatt had prayed with me to be baptised in the Spirit. Yet my working life was not fully satisfying. And I still longed for God's restoration which He had promised me.

I was going to teach at a men's weekend south of Paris. God had given me a particular message on 'entering His rest' from the Epistle to the Hebrews. I had been brought to the place of answered prayer; of truly trusting God. The weekend went well from the start. An earnest young Frenchman came to me at the beginning of my first session to tell me there was a spirit of lust in the meeting. Being a respectable Englishman, I wasn't quite sure what to do about this, but I knew I could not ignore it. So, when I finished, I very quickly mentioned it, offered prayer, and then dismissed the group of about three hundred, for a wine and coffee break. They all seemed to stay for prayer. I was overwhelmed by Frenchmen. The final session was on the Saturday morning. God said to me, 'You will pray for all the men individually, before you fly home.' This was impossible; I was due to catch the plane after lunch from Paris, in order to get home in time to speak to a youth group in Frome. He said, 'All you will need to do is to speak the name of Jesus.'

Overnight I practised, 'Au nom de Jesus.' The next day, having delivered the talk, I invited men who wished for prayer, to come forward – firstly from one block of the auditorium; they all stood up and came forward. I got them into lines, and went towards the first man. Without touching him I said, 'Au nom de Jesus,' and he fell backwards as the Holy Spirit came upon him. As I walked down the row, and spoke the name of Jesus, it kept happening this way. Within ten minutes it seemed that everyone, including the leaders who had been with me, had the same experience. There was no emotionalism, just peace and a strong smell of garlic!

A few weeks later, I experienced a similar thing at an FGBMFI convention at Hull University. It was at the evening dinner that I spoke on the same theme. The guests stood to receive God's blessing. After praying, I opened my eyes and was astounded to see smartly dressed people lying all over the floor. Again, there was another similar experience at a convention in Swindon a few weeks later. What a powerful message, and a tremendous sense of God's presence and peace.

'When are you going to receive this for yourself?' God said. And I did. Within days, a job as Assistant to the Chief Executive of Avon County was advertised. A promotion, without any need to relocate, and to a job most like the opportunity in Birmingham seven years before.

It was a new experience to be the oldest on the short list, rather than the youngest. The youngest was an excellent woman candidate who later became a Chief Executive Officer, and a good friend. Avon was a highly political Council, with many able and articulate members who would later move on to be Members of Parliament. The social aspect of the interview process was quite unstructured, but I had learnt my lesson and, when the formal interview progressed easily, and the answers to questions came readily to mind, I knew this was God's direction. I readily accepted the job offered to me.

God does not waste anything in your experience. The job of developing the Corporate Policy Review Unit and, for a time, helping to direct and implement the Council's computer strategy, put to good use the experience I had gained in Wiltshire.

It was amazing to see how different was the culture of the two neighbouring Councils. There was the shock of having to contend with Bristol traffic. My solution was to make an early start and to arrive at the office by 7.30 a.m. The problem was that, at the other end of the day, I faced the same traffic, and this usually meant long days away from home.

This was to be a marvellous experience of working for a Christian Chief Executive Officer. Neville Pearce had been the youngest Chief Executive in the country when he had earlier worked for Bath City Council. Now he was undertaking one of the most testing jobs outside London. An impressive man in every way, he taught me vital lessons about how to work in a highly-charged political environment. Despite the pressures, he always had time for people and was genuinely concerned for their well-being. The office cleaner, for example, was greeted by name. Neville was a man of his word, who could be totally trusted; a role model of a Christian working at the highest level, whose life was marked by commitment and integrity. Working with him was stimulating, especially supporting the Chief Officers' management team. It was a huge organisation, with thirty-five thousand staff and spending £650 million a year. We introduced performance indicators, took initiatives on community safety, gave a lead on equal opportunities, and developed a new computing strategy.

Over the years we had had so many near misses, or failures, at moving house, that I was determined we should make a move! Every time you move, it requires faith. There will always be unknowns. And when I discovered a converted barn, I knew this was the right one. We jumped in with an offer which was accepted, with a demand for an early settlement. We went ahead, and put our house on the market. All this was fine, until we went out to dinner with a couple who, over dinner, asked about our house and we explained the step we had taken – and that we were committed to a bridging loan. They responded that, having taken similar action some time before, they had been nearly bankrupted.

I left their home in fear and panic, determined that I had to deal urgently with our situation.

We were to discover, some months later, what made me act irrationally and so to lose out financially on a move we never made. It was a vital lesson to be learnt that, when God speaks to you through his Word, the Bible, it is essential to act. We visited friends in Worcester, Dr and Mrs Calcot and received clear direction as we prayed about our situation. The guidance was that we should move. Yet still I could not. I was now gripped by a fear, which was fuelled by the crash in the stock market, in which I had invested in a minor way. More importantly, we discovered that a girl, who had turned up at the Rectory in our village parish, had gone back to her occult group in Devon, putting a curse on all those who had tried to help her. The result was a whole range of problems for a number of friends including the Rector and, for me, a cloud of confusion. When we were told what had happened, this lifted immediately – but I was left feeling foolish and exhausted. Work was now full of challenges. With Hilary's support I was able to put this trauma behind me, and could not wait to get going again on my career.

The CVs went out regularly and I hit the interview trail again. My expertise in interview techniques and psychometric tests improved by the month. One of the closest where I came to being appointed was in a smart outer London borough. There was one problem. They wanted me to do a graphology test. The problem was that Hilary said I shouldn't, because it would not honour God. I phoned a friend, hoping that he would say this could be an exception. His wife answered the telephone, and the question was put to her. The answer was only slightly less clear. She said, 'No!' Having proven I could eat properly, and do the psychometric (including numeracy) tests, all that was left was the final interview. The inevitable question came from the Chairman.

'Why will you not do a graphology test?'

'Because I am a Christian and if you cannot take me on my performance over the three days, my references, and track record, you need to look elsewhere.' They did!

It is often only when we come to the end of our own resources that God can act. I had indeed reached that point. Driving into Bristol the next day, a question came into my mind, as I waited at a set of traffic lights. 'What is the objective of your life?' This was an easy question to answer at the start of the day. Some years previously, I had attended a management course, at Brunel University, in place of the Director. I faced the same question in the opening session. This was easy to deal with, because I had thought the matter through when teaching management by objectives to Christian businessmen. At Brunel, I wrote down my answer, thinking this was simply a thought-provoking opener. The facilitator then said, 'I want you to pair up and explain your objective to the other person.' I thought, 'How do I rewrite this in two minutes, so as to appear normal?' The woman Director of Social Services of a London Borough sat opposite me. I could not ask her to go first, yet if I didn't it was rude. So there I sat, a perplexed middle-aged white male, not sure what to do. She asked me to go first.

'You may not understand this, but the objective of my life is to glorify God.'

Her eyes widened. She said, 'Tell me more.' For the next half hour I talked to her about Jesus. We never found time to discuss her objectives.

The next question came to mind.

'What are your priorities?' Again, a straightforward start to the day.

'You come first – fellowship with God, then the family – Hilary, Peter and Victoria, then work, followed by Christian activity, and recreation.'

'Full points,' I thought. Then came another question.

'Does Hilary want to leave Bath?'

'Of course not. She loves it here, and so do the children. All her friends are here, and so is her work.'

'Why, then, are you applying for jobs all over the country?' In seconds I had gone through this process and, as the lights changed, I once again had to offer my career back to God, affirming that Hilary and the children were more important than my pursuing my ambition.

It was with a great sense of peace that I entered my office on the seventh floor of Avon House. When the secretaries came in, an hour and a half later, I was ready to tell them I was happy to be at Avon House for the next twelve years. They showed some relief that my period of dashing off to interviews was over but, for some reason, did not seem as excited as I was.

A few weeks previously, Hilary had told me that God had spoken to her, telling her that I was going back to Wiltshire. It sounded so improbable that I had ignored her comment. Three days after giving up my ambition, I found myself speaking with Trevor Partridge at a training weekend organised for the Christian staff of a major financial services company. On arrival at the conference venue, the secretary, who had only been a Christian a relatively short time, told me that she had been prompted, that very week, to look at the public appointments page of the *Independent* newspaper. In the centre of the page a job was advertised for a Chief Executive of West Wiltshire District Council. She said, 'God told me it was your job if you applied.' It was hard to concentrate during the weekend which followed.

On Monday, there was another telephone call, prompting the same action – this time from a non Christian. God can sometimes give His guidance through non Christians. On the Wednesday I said, 'Father, I bet you couldn't do that a third time.' The telephone rang straight away. It was another friend from Trowbridge, who repeated the same message!

Nine

ROOM AT THE TOP

Trowbridge was the town in which I had worked for most of my career. The first time, in 1965, the prospect of working there was not, on first impressions, very exciting. In 1989, I went with a great sense of expectation. Just because God has given clear indications about potential success does not mean that you should not prepare thoroughly to make a professional job of the interview. By this time, I was experienced in all aspects of the assessment process. It was done well, and seemed very professional. The interview flowed easily. My policy is always to be open, honest and myself. If they don't like you, it is best not to get the job. They did like me, and I was offered the appointment.

My ambition of becoming a Chief Executive was fulfilled when I took up the position in July. The management structure had been reorganised before I arrived, so there appeared to be no difficult organisational issues to tackle, although it was an unusual approach to adopt unless an internal appointment was expected.

Having got into the habit of early starts to beat the traffic to Bristol, I continued to get up early and because of the ease of the drive to Trowbridge, was in most mornings at 7.00 a.m. and sometimes earlier. I started the day reading my Bible, and praying for wisdom for me, the staff and members of the council. The day was planned, priorities sorted and I was able to get on with my priority tasks before the telephone and meetings caused me to follow other people's agendas.

The council had been renowned for the successful sale of software to other councils and to be a leader in privatisation and embracing competition. The software business had been transferred out of the authority to a separate company prior to my starting, as had the legal services. Questions about these transfers were being put to me by the press and by staff, who would give me documents to read. They were also asking about a property company that the council had established and I thought that the only way to settle these matters was to give open answers as the objective new boy. My enquiries and reading of the papers failed to satisfy me or the press. When I discovered that leading councillors may not have appreciated the full implications of some of the decisions they had taken, after taking informal advice with the District Auditor and the Chartered Institute of Public Finance and Accountancy I had to recommend that he should undertake an independent investigation. This was agreed by Members but on the day the auditor came into the office to start his work, I was suspended.

It was a very unreal situation. My apparent challenge to what had gone on immediately prior to my arrival had caused great consternation amongst a small group of members and staff, but I was in an impossible position where for me to do nothing with my experience of management buy-outs and computing would no doubt have led to personal criticism, had I failed to take appropriate action. Although I had only taken a superficial look at things it was evident from my previous experience that the situation was full of potential conflicts of interest. The need for independent advice seemed not to have been appreciated, and the full range of information necessary for members to objectively consider the alternatives may have resulted in the council's interests not being properly protected.

When my secretary ran down the corridor to tell me of my pending suspension, my first reaction was to get all relevant and personal papers out of the office and into the car. It was all very unreal and when the three senior councillors came to see me, the one thought that came to mind was, 'Pick up your papers and walk out with dignity.' They may have expected a confrontation but after listening to them, I simply said that it was sad things had come to this, and walked out.

'You won't believe what has just happened,' I said to Hilary, arriving at our converted barn. (We did get one in the end) 'I have been suspended.'

'Praise God! Isn't that exciting,' she said. Here was my career at an end, and this is the response I got! A few minutes later, Ken

Franks, the local producer for BBC Wiltshire Sound, rang to say, 'Did you forget you were giving us an interview at 5.15 p.m.?' I apologised, and he then asked me, 'Have you been suspended?' I had given him no hint of my situation, but my policy is always to be honest and I had to say, 'yes'– and so the story hit the media the next day.

In the morning I went to see a good friend, the Chief Executive of the County, Andy Browning, and we went out for lunch together. He advised that I should speak to a man called Bill Miles, a former Chief Executive, who advised Chief Executives in trouble. Driving back to the village, the HTV van was in the lane and although I tried to look nonchalant they spotted me and I gave my first interview in the garden.

The first person to visit me the next day was the Rector of our village church, Derek Smith. We walked together alongside the Kennet & Avon Canal, which we overlook from our home. Bill Miles gave me unexpected advice on handling the media, which proved to be absolutely right. He advised to go for full media exposure as it was impossible to continue to work in the situation and I needed to get everyone behind me. So the house was full of reporters and camera men right up to the Friday on which a small group of members would determine my future. One councillor who was a friend from my County Council days, and also a highly respected member of the District Council, Tony Phillips O.B.E., briefed himself to argue my cause. One of the criticisms made of me was that of my seeing too much of backbench members, particularly the difficult ones. My response had been that I had a legal duty in respect of every councillor and I had to exercise that properly. Tony who was to become Chairman of the Council was to play a major role in the restoration of the council and its standing with the public. What was to have as great, if not greater, impact that afternoon was that most of the staff walked out to support me during the meeting. I knew nothing of this and was deeply moved to see on television the staff with their placards outside the District Council Offices.

The dining room had been turned into a television studio. We were to go live on the early evening news when the decision on my future had been made. I was to be reinstated on the Monday. The telephone had not stopped ringing all week. We had to buy an answering machine to get a break. On the following Monday the cameras followed me back to the office and into a large staff meeting I called to thank my colleagues for their support and to promise that the audit investigation would be completed. I had no idea of what the detailed investigation would reveal or that it would lead to three major public interest reports, and also a series of serious Ombudsman reports all of which would require my action. The most telling action taken on the advice of our solicitors was that of bringing to an end our relationship with the computer software company because they deemed it to be unlawful. As a result the company went into liquidation. Within twenty-four hours the business was back under the management of the council. It was run successfully and in its final year under the control of the council made £2.5 million profit and was sold to a facilities management company called CAPITA for £4 million.

The work of actioning the audit reports took a lot of time and delayed my plans to improve the performance of the council. What had happened had not been good for the reputation of local government, and a high priority was to restore public confidence in the council. Every morning I started the day praying for wisdom, and for the staff and councillors. We restructured the organisation and, without exception, staff responded to new responsibilities with great relish. New staff joined the authority, bringing just the skills we needed. The Press and Marketing Officer was one such person, and one of a number of highly successful women appointed to senior positions during this time. There was a new culture of openness and a high investment in staff development. We were to be one of the first local authorities to achieve Investor in People status for the whole authority. It was also essential to buy in the right consultancy expertise and, time and time again, I was given wisdom in making this selection.

Elections brought about major changes on the council, the majority of members being new. There was a change of political leadership, and we quickly drafted a Corporate Plan around the Liberal Democrat manifesto. The new leader of the council was a committed Christian, as were the leaders of the other political groups. It was remarkable that after a full debate all forty-three members in a politically diverse council unanimously endorsed the Corporate Plan. Each year, we measured performance against the Plan. Although we faced difficult times and decisions, services to the public were increased and performance improved year by year, as we made significant savings, reducing the staff by about twenty percent. In 1993 I was a finalist for the prize for Public Management Leadership. These were rewarding years, and were successful because of the high quality team of staff and the willingness of a very committed group of councillors to work together for the good of the community.

There was no doubt these were times of intense pressure and long hours heightened by a police investigation, constant media attention involving regular television and radio interviews, and a stream of complex and technical matters to deal with in managing a software business and preparing for its sale. Neville Pearce had joked that I would do the job in two days a week. How little did he or I appreciate what I was going into. Providentially, I had been given such a clear word from the Bible the morning I had to call in the auditors, I never doubted or had any anxiety about the eventual outcome.

One of the most important lessons of my time in West Wiltshire was the importance of forgiveness. You cannot afford to hold anything against anyone, no matter how much they may have seemed to be hostile to you. Some of the most amazing healings I have seen have been in the context of forgiveness, and a number of exciting stories come racing into my mind. One of the most special was that of the wife of the pastor of a church south of Paris. God sent what I would describe as angelic physiotherapists to minister to her – something I have seen on a number of occasions, and which never ceases to amaze me.

More than forgiveness, it was essential to speak God's blessings over those who were against me, and this was brought home to me when I was speaking at a church weekend at Buckfastleigh on the theme of praise. There was one particular problem I had inherited which affected a member of the community who had felt aggrieved by the actions of the council.

I did everything possible to resolve the dispute fairly, with the result that I was criticised for a problem which was not of my creation. God challenged me to praise Him even in this situation – and I did, otherwise my teaching weekend would have been hypocritical. Within three days a settlement was reached and the matter concluded. How did it happen? Praise was God's answer, not clever negotiation.

An even more remarkable incident occurred as a result of my testifying about the importance of forgiveness, at a meeting for businessmen, in Belgium. A man at the meeting had been accused of misappropriating a sum of money. Even his wife was beginning to believe that he had done it, though he continued to protest his innocence. Listening to me, he decided to exercise his will to forgive those who were wrongly accusing him. The next morning he telephoned the person I was staying with, to recount a remarkable story. After he had forgiven, whilst sitting at the dinner table, God put into his mind a picture of a bank account, which showed an entry for the missing sum of money. As he looked at the account, both the name of the account holder and the account number became clear. He knew where the money had gone, and could clear his name.

In all this tension there was the enjoyment of achieving things for the community. Public service can still provide a great sense of satisfaction. There were enough light-hearted moments for me to write a local government version of 'Yes Minister'. Minor ambitions were also fulfilled. I wanted to have my name on a plaque, to announce election results, and to go to Grimsby. Within a few months I had a call from the new Principal of the highly regarded Trowbridge Technical College. Would I be prepared to do the official opening of their new computer wing? I accepted instantly, but tried to sound nonchalant. The day came and, in front of the invited guests and press, did my little speech. To the kind of one-handed applause you get when people are holding drinks, I pulled the cord. Too embarrassed to see if they had got the name right, I slipped back later to make sure. Next came an election, and I fulfilled the important role of Returning Officer that I had witnessed in Wolverhampton Civic Hall when helping with the counting of votes. 'I, the Returning Officer....' The candidate who lost made a typical 'why I lost' speech and it was so rewarding to see democracy at work.

When my very able Secretary, Mary, who gave me loyal support in managing the council, told me I had a call from Grimsby to undertake a speaking engagement, I asked her to book me a flight. She was impressed, and told me the flights were either in the afternoon or early evening. The thought came strongly to book the evening flight, even though I would miss the dinner. The question you are bound to be asking is, 'Why Grimsby?' There was this advertisement I had seen in a business magazine. It was a full page picture of an evidently happy and glamorous family on a superb yacht coursing its way through the water. Underneath the caption read, 'This man rediscovered his family – he moved to Grimsby.' When the day of the dinner came, my PA (a Christian) came to me, concerned that the leading Members had called for a meeting at four o'clock, for which my presence was essential. Now I understood why the evening flight had been the right one to book. I prepared a paper so that a quick decision could be made. They welcomed the paper, made a decision, and then spent time discussing it.

It was on the way in to the short term car park at Heathrow that I did something I never do. Yes, I prayed for a car parking space! It was desperate as it was 7.20 and the flight was due to leave at 7.30. The first place was empty, and I reversed straight in. It was a run to the terminal and through security. In my haste, I took the wrong turn, to be stopped by an angel. She worked for Aer Lingus. Following her directions, I got to the check-in point, putting my ticket on the counter.

'The flight has just closed Mr Latham, I am sorry.' There was only one thing to do, and that was to pray. In these circumstances I tend not to kneel, or close my eyes, in case people think I have gone to sleep. Silently, I prayed. 'You want me to be in Grimsby tonight. Please do something about it.' With that a bus pulled up outside the door and a man dashed in.

'I left one of my bags at security. Can I go back to collect it?

'No sir, we will put it on the morning flight.' She tore out my flight coupon,saying, 'Mr Latham, have a good flight.' That night a number of businessmen committed their lives to Christ and after catching the early morning plane, I was back at my desk for a 9.00 a.m. start the next day.

My purpose for being at the office was to work, but you cannot hide your Christian faith. Staff would come for prayer, before the start of the working day. When, at the height of the problems, the Bishop came to the office to pray with me, Mary recounted how she felt a presence go through the room. No he was not wearing a funny hat, or carrying a crook! She, along with others, put their careers on the line to support me – not because I am a Christian, but simply because I was someone trying to do the right thing. It was after a few years working together that Mary was behaving strangely one Monday morning. I hoped I had not upset her in some way. I had been there since early morning and it was now 6.20. She came to my room and, taking a deep breath, said, 'Mr Latham, I became like you yesterday.'

I looked for signs of an operation, which were not evident, and said, 'Do tell me.' Mary had been taken to church and, on hearing about Jesus, had made her own personal commitment to Christ. I thought, 'Oh good, another secretary to spend eternity with.'

Sitting at my desk one day, my meeting with my brilliant woman Head of Computing was interrupted by a telephone call from a doctor in Somerset. I asked if I could take the call, pressing the button so it came through on the speaker.

'Don Latham?' he said.

'Yes.'

'My brother came to hear you at Shepton Mallet Parish Church last week at a healing service. He became a Christian and was completely healed of his cancer.'

'It was rather a good night,' I said, rather tamely, trying not to look across the desk. I never impose my faith on people, especially at work, but in my experience it is impossible to keep good news quiet.

It was now all going so well, and then God spoke to me clearly, to tell me it was time to move on.

'You have dwelt long enough on this mountain. Go in and possess the land,' was the verse that stood out of the page on my daily reading that Good Friday. I had learned the lesson that it is vitally important to do what God tells you, but I did ask for confirmation, and on the Sunday we went to Bath City Church (not our regular place of worship). Part way through a time of praise, a man walked to the microphone to say that God had given him a word for someone. It was Julian, who had taken me to Los Angeles. Looking, it seemed, straight at me, at the back of the large church which meets in an art deco restored cinema, he confirmed what God had already shown me from the Bible. A second confirmation was to come the next day, from Pastor Janet Woods, a great friend who prayed for us regularly. God had spoken to her in her morning time of intercession.

It would seem impossible to go wrong with such clear direction – but I did. My ambition had been to follow the Chief Executive's role with a national position. I had been on the professional council of my Institute, CIPFA, for three years during my time as Assistant County Treasurer in Wiltshire County Council, and hoped that I would end up in a national position of some influence. When the post of Director of the Local Government Management Board was advertised I thought, this is it. But it was to prove that things from my previous experience still needed dealing with before I would be ready for such an appointment.

Ten

LEARNING FROM FAILURE

I had been successful. From office junior, making tea in Wolverhampton Town Hall, I had arrived at the position of Chief Executive of West Wiltshire District Council. The attitude of hard work, always trying to give my best, learning from others, and asking God for wisdom had, despite all my fears and weaknesses, got me through to the top. I was once asked, in an interview, what the key to my success was. The instant response I gave was, 'He who honours God, God will honour.

For years, over half my holiday time had been spent in travel to speak at Christian meetings and conferences. But, although this was a sacrifice, in terms of time with the family forgone, there had been many wonderful times in the UK, Ireland, Europe, America and the Caribbean. It was amazing how one engagement often led to another, and life had brought some remarkable experiences. God is no man's debtor.

I saw the blind receive their sight, the crippled walk, the deaf hear, and many wonderful answers to prayer. Hilary often had to stay at home with the children, and was frequently given words of knowledge, about people's needs in the meeting and churches in which I was speaking. These were always so accurate, and we ministered together, despite being in different places.

I was always careful to ensure that my Christian activity was separate from work. As Chief Executive, I worked at least fifty hours a week, and more during the crisis years. It was inevitable that staff would find out about my faith – including coming to hear the 'boss' speak when I was preaching – or listening to my doing the Thought for the Day on Wiltshire Sound. The challenge is always to live up to what you say – to 'walk the talk'.

Again, you would think that, with all this evidence, and experience of God's power, that I would have been able to face any challenge. But it is one thing to know God for His power, and another thing to know Him as Father. If I were to be asked for the priority for any new Christian, it would be to get to know God as Father. This is what makes Christianity unique. We believe that through Jesus, the Son of God, you can get to know God as Father. Not a distant cosmic policeman, who is always looking for ways of punishing you but, 'Abba, Father' – Daddy. Jesus came to reveal the Father to mankind. I was going to have to go through some painful times to come into an awareness of that reality for myself. Without realising it, we tend to base our concept of God on our experiences of our relationship, or lack of it, with our human father. This is almost inevitably faulty in some degree, and it takes time, and a healing process, to put it right. God was going to use another failure to get me to address the issue. It is not enough to know the power of God. This does not give you security. You have to know Him personally, and to learn to understand His ways.

I felt trapped into applying for a job I was unsure about. I wanted to work in London – not Luton. If you are ill prepared for interview, and not clear that you want a job and that you have thought through the issues, you will not get it – certainly at the top level. And I didn't. When the phone call came through, and this was confirmed, I felt disconsolate. The guidance had been so clear, and I had failed. One thing that I had learned is that God, who knows the end from the beginning, had prepared for this situation. But facts tell you that you have blown your one and only opportunity. Instead of whingeing, I went to those who knew me, for prayer. How could I be sorted out, so that I would be successful next time? The trusted friends all had the same advice, and the last person who came to our house had no idea of the circumstances. Pastor John Solly said,

'God put it in your heart to apply for that job so that He might expose everything that is in your heart that would be working against you when you went for the job that God ultimately has for you,' "...to humble you and test you, to know what was in your heart"' Deut 8:2. (NKJV)

I knew it was true. Through prayer, study and experience over the next few months, I came into a new understanding of God as Father. When a new job, as the first Director of SOLACE (Society of Local Authority Chief Executives), was advertised, I knew this would be everything that I hoped for. This time there would be no mistakes. I would be thoroughly prepared, and ready for any question. It was a straightforward process, with forty-five minutes of rigorous questioning, as you would expect from a group of top Chief Executives – and I was offered the part-time post.

The majority of councillors understood my desire to move on, and to have such a post, even though it was to be on a short term and part-time basis. It was not only an honour for me, but also recognition for the council. Before leaving, I recommended an internal reorganisation and appointment, which would make further savings for the council. It would have been easy to have settled down. The hard work had been done. Regrettably, my competitive nature always needs a fresh challenge. I wanted to leave when I still had more to offer, had not lost my enthusiasm for the job, and when people didn't want me to go. That is just what happened and I must admit missing colleagues who had been so loyal to me, and became friends, which was one of the many advantages of a comparatively small organisation. The West Wiltshire staff and members were an exceptional group at that time, and I am glad things went on from strength to strength.

SOLACE was all that I had hoped for. We were made so welcome by Sam Jones, Town Clerk of the Corporation of London, the President for the year, and by his wife Jean. On my first day in the Kensington & Chelsea Office, where the Secretary Alan Taylor the Chief Executive, and small administrative team, were based, I had a call from the BBC.

'Does a local authority need a Chief Executive?' was the question. I gave my first television interview in the Westminster Studio that day, with a picture of the Palace of Westminster behind me. It was a great privilege to be working with some of the most talented and committed people in public service.

Working from home on a self-employed basis required new discipline, and I was not good at it. There is no such thing as a part-time job, and we found ourselves working six days a week. The Saturday post was not left until Monday; it was at least looked at on Saturday. The study door should have been closed at six o'clock – but it wasn't. Every week required a minimum of a day in London, often two or three. This is where the contacts were, and the network had to be established and maintained. The main office was at Kensington and Chelsea, so I could stay with my sister Diane, and enjoy the delights of Marylebone High Street. The main challenge was to draw up a business plan, setting out a future direction for the Society, and to make the views of the Society more forcefully known. This, in my view, required constant contact with members at a personal level and at regional group meetings. I was keen to represent their views on all aspects of the work of the Society. Being self-employed, I had agreed to meet all the costs of undertaking the role, including all travel and office expenses. However, I really enjoyed the regular contact with the media and members, giving informal advice. My hope was that a permanent office would be established in London, and that the job would develop into a full-time post, for which I would be considered. Sadly, it was not to be, and the contract did not run its possible three year term. The office moved from London to Knowsley, and to work effectively part-time from three centres so far apart proved impractical. There were also differences in perception about how the role of Director should be carried out, and about how the Society should function, which emerged from a change in leadership.

From never talking about work at home, self-employment had, for the first time, brought Hilary and me together in work. The job could not be done without a PA. The telephone rang continually. Correspondence had to be dealt with and activities organised. So, when I went to a meeting of senior officers of the Society, to review the situation the week following our annual conference in Sheffield, I naturally took Hilary. It was a shock for her more than me when I was asked to make way for a full-time appointment, to be made in Knowsley. We had no wish to move north at that time. The Society had moved on rapidly and it was seen to be essential to have a Director who could physically work more closely with the Secretary and staff. The positive side was that the initial agenda set out for me had been successfully completed ahead of schedule, and a letter was sent from the Society to the council thanking them for releasing me to take on the role, albeit for a shorter time than originally expected.

I cannot say that I would have stayed at West Wiltshire, had I known this would happen, because I knew I had given that job all I could. More importantly, God had shown so clearly that it was time to move on to new things, and I had no intention of repeating past mistakes. It had been another ambition to experience self-employment, but I would not recommend it to others unless you have clearly thought through the issues, and as a Christian, have had real confirmation that it is right for you.

Eleven

GOD IS FAITHFUL

Within a few days of the eventful meeting in Sheffield, a more significant thing happened. We all take our health for granted – until something goes wrong. What I noticed as I walked from the bathroom to my bedroom in my sister's house in London, was that one of my testicles was swollen. My immediate reaction was to ask God, in prayer, what was the cause and how to deal with it.

I telephoned home before starting out on my schedule for the day. Hilary reminded me of some books we needed for our Alpha Group, and that she wanted me to buy a book on heaven that she had seen previously in Wesley Owen bookshop, Wigmore Street. She described exactly where the book was located in the shop. After breakfast in Pret a Manger, in Marylebone High Street, I walked to the bookshop.

As I looked for Hilary's book, my eye was drawn to a book on unbroken curses. I instinctively knew that it contained the answer to my prayer earlier that morning. Bending down, I saw Hilary's book on heaven. Having bought them and the Alpha books, I made my way to the Australian embassy, to get our visas for our planned summer holiday. We were going to Fiji, via Bangkok and Australia, as a special trip to celebrate our thirtieth wedding anniversary. The embassy ran a very efficient system of queuing – a bit like getting your tickets in the delicatessen in Waitrose, where you meet such nice people. As I waited, I sat and read my book, confident it contained the answer. Visas in my briefcase, I walked along the Embankment in the Spring sunshine. There was time for coffee before walking on to Westminster for my working lunch. It was as I sat in the cafe that the answer came. There was an unbroken curse of sickness over our family, which had led to the early deaths of my father, his brother, and my brother, David.

My mind went back to the death of David, a few years earlier. We had not seen each other for some time and, when I did see him, he had that drawn look of someone whose life was being drained away. He had lost weight and, in some ways, looked like the man I had stood alongside at his wedding as his best man. But, when I prayed for his healing and baptism in the Spirit, I found it hard to exercise faith. He had so longed to get better so that he could join me in telling others about Jesus. Mother called me at the office a few days later to say that David had found himself praying in a strange language when on the loo. Was this all right? Isn't it good that the one and only true God is not religious! David had been put off walking in his Christian faith but, in these final weeks of his earthly life, his faith – which he came into at St. Luke's – came flooding back, and he was such an encouragement to those who cared for him, his family and friends. The funeral at St. Luke's had been a celebration.

I had prayed for so many people to be cut free from things of heredity, the things of former generations, often with immediate and spectacular results. Why had I not asked someone to do this for me? There is the danger in spending all your time ministering to other people that you do not give time to receiving the help you need yourself.

When God shows you a need, He also prepares the way for it to be dealt with. For me, that was to receive prayer from the Reverend Paul Hoffman, who was visiting a church in Warminster the following Sunday. More important even than asking for prayer is hearing God speak. It is what God speaks into the situation that transforms it. The way He speaks is through His Word – the Bible.

'I shall not die, but live, and declare the works of the Lord' Psalm 118:17. (NKJV)

That was my reading the next day. The logos – the general Word – became 'rhema' – living and specific to me, and I know that when God has spoken a word He will perform it.

Over the next weeks and months, God was going to confirm His word time and time again. In June, I ministered in a church on the edge of Liverpool's Chinatown. A wonderful church

Liverpool Christian Life Centre – where should you leave your car outside, you are likely to find that, if it is still there after the service, it will be minus its wheels! Then, on Saturday, I was in a church plant in Cheshire, pastored by Gill Freeney. It was at her church on the Sunday morning that at the end, whilst the church was praying for me, a woman had a picture in her imagination of a ball coming out of me. I love God's sense of humour! She had no idea I had anything wrong with me. The following month, we were visiting friends for supper with a Peruvian pastor and his wife. Giving a blessing over the guests after a meal, he prayed in Spanish for my intimate parts to be healed! This was fine until the prayer was interpreted into English! During this time, God gave three separate people words of knowledge about the future which He was planning for us.

Despite all the words of encouragement, the symptoms became worse. Your mind gets full of crazy ideas and you imagine all kinds of pains. I should have gone to the doctor, but I didn't. We were now about to make the trip of a lifetime. Two Canadian guests visited us on the day we were due to travel, and we entertained them by taking them on the open top bus around our beautiful city of Bath. It was a trip we had always thought of doing, but had never got round to. This was followed by lunch, and our visitors were impressed. As I packed, thoughts came flooding into the mind. 'How foolish to go to the other side of the world in your state of health, etc.' It was when I was opening the post that God gave assurance that everything would be all right. Noel Pizzey, the first person I had prayed for from work to be baptised in the Spirit, had written to me. During the weekend, he had a dream. It was so vivid he had felt compelled to write to tell me. In the dream, he had come to our house. He asked God to tell him why he had come.

'You are to tell him, God is faithful.' When God speaks, it is so clear and so simple. Bangkok is an amazing city. We wanted to go back to the Sheraton, especially the Thai restaurant, and to the shops to buy more silks. The traffic is appalling, but the people are charming. The Thai women are so beautiful and the city, particularly the river, buzzes with life. We had tea in the Writer's Wing at the Oriental Hotel. There was a memorable elegance about the place as the quartet played their chamber music. Sydney,

Australia, is a city we have re-visited a number of times. We were so impressed as we walked around the well-known circular quay to the opera house to see people dining outdoors, in the middle of the Australian winter. At night I was attacked by fear and could not sleep – but the next day we took our flight to Fiji.

It is hard to describe the next week, which was to be one of the most memorable of a lifetime. The hotel on the main island was good but, as we drove to catch our seaplane to Turtle Island, I had the feeling we were in for something special, as we saw whole families walking alongside the road on the way to church. Four of us packed into the little plane, which we physically rocked at one point as we sped across the water towards land. Then, with air under the wings, we took off across an ocean of wonderful variations of blue, seeing a coral reef just below the water, and islands dotted about in the way in the way only a perfect designer could achieve.

As the plane descended towards the island, we could see the welcoming party on the beach. Completing the landing, with the noise of the engine falling, suddenly we could hear the welcome songs. Wading through warm clear water, we were given an unforgettable reception to this wonderful island which accommodates only twenty-eight guests. Fourteen couples for fourteen beaches – which you can book for the day. Va, the manageress, took us to our beach house (bura). It was beautiful, and it even had a jacuzzi. We later gathered in the cocktail lounge, a flattened area of sand surrounded by colourful bushes, to meet other guests and to have a pre-dinner drink. The conversations flowed. Most guests were from Australia, New Zealand and the west coast of America. Young, successful business people or, like us, those with grown-up families, who had the finances and freedom to travel. Niumah the head waiter smiled. All the staff smiled, and then Niumah told us that our dinner was now ready.

'We have a custom on the island. We always give thanks for our meals.' He then introduced another member of staff, who gave thanks in Fijian. I was thinking that this must be the only five star hotel in the world that does this. As we sat enjoying our meal, seated around the long table on the beach, staff were singing with their guitars. Some were Fijian songs but I could hardly believe my ears when the next song in English was, 'All over the world the Spirit is moving', followed by a second verse, 'All over Fiji, the Spirit is moving'.

We were in a Christian country, and were to discover that the majority of the staff were committed Christians. Sunday afternoon entertainment for the guests consisted of the children and Chief from the neighbouring island coming over to sing Christian choruses. There was something special about the place – not only the physical beauty, but the presence of God, could be seen in the people, who were always singing, smiling and giving their best in excellent service. This was truly a foretaste of heaven. On the first night I prayed that God would take my pain away, so that I could enjoy the holiday – and the pain went instantly. When we were quickly discovered to be Christians, I was soon asked to give thanks for the meal. The look on the other guests' faces when I was introduced as 'brother Don' was an absolute picture! It always amazes me that, just because you can articulate your faith, other people think you must be a professional clergyman. I often get called 'Rev' without having had the ordination! On the Sunday we went to church on the next island, and it seemed that 80% of the population were there. I thought how wonderful it would be if the UK became a Christian nation again, and we could see a thousand Christians in our village.

We were upgraded for the final leg home from Los Angeles to London, but the pain came back and I decided to go to the doctor. He took one look at my cricket ball and said it was a hydrocele, which needed an operation or a miracle. He could believe for a miracle, but after discussion said he would start off the long process leading to an operation. In fact, the National Health Service responded more quickly than expected. The young consultant confirmed my doctor's diagnosis, but said they would do a scan as a precaution. It was the scan, a few weeks later, which gave the doctor cause for concern. There was a dark patch, and he recommended urgent action, and not to wait for the planned day surgery. Over the next month it was good to have words of confirmation that everything would be all right, especially as the consultant thought that this could be the early stages of a tumour and was 'a chance find', which should not spread to other parts of the body.

The word that God kept on repeating was, 'God is faithful.'

Having spoken at a meeting in our village hall, I was driving back to an ICCC (International Christian Chamber of Commerce) conference in Sussex. A friend, a former colleague, had given me a batch of tapes to listen to. I picked out one as I drove away, asking that it would be God's word to me. 'God is faithful' was the subject the speaker had chosen!

It was now early December 1996. I was about to be released from another fear – that of hospitals. Hilary drove me down to Royal United Hospital, Bath and I joined the other men in the small ward. They were mainly in for prostate operations, and we went through the preparatory checks. Being wheeled to an X-ray was another new experience. Being told I had to go in for a second picture, because there appeared to be a problem, was disconcerting, to say the least. But God had even provided for that. One of our best friends was not due on duty that day, but was in the hospital, and spotted us in the corridor.

'Why are you looking so worried?' she said. Hearing what had happened, she said that she would find out. Professionally she could not, and did not tell us, but when she returned she was smiling, and that was a great relief. Hilary was with me all day, and walked alongside the trolley as I was wheeled to theatre wearing my long white stockings. A man with a beard leant over me and we had a brief conversation. The superb male nurse confirmed my decision to have a full anaesthetic. After about sixteen seconds the bearded man turned into a beautiful nurse asking me if I felt OK. This was a miracle on the National Health Service, and so different from my childhood memories of having my tonsils removed!

My publisher had given me a book by Adrian Plass, to read in hospital. It caused me some pain, as laughing pulled the stitches. Truly, what it means to be in stitches! Next morning, the young doctor sat on my bed and explained that it was a growth they had taken out. I would most probably have to come back after Christmas – and after our week of skiing. He explained the treatment that I might need, and the possible degree of success. It all seemed a bit unreal, but the male nurse was terrific, as were all the staff. I thought how much more difficult was his job than mine had been as Chief Executive of a local authority. A week later, I attended a meeting called Coffee Pot in Bristol. There I was called up by Evelyn Angel, who ran these excellent meetings, to help her pray for others. One man returned to his seat after prayer. A few minutes later, he was back in front of me.

'I have never done this before, but God just spoke to me and told me to tell you that – "all is well".'

This was a wonderful send-off for our week's skiing holiday, when I was to serve as Chaplain to Verbier. Two weeks from the operation, I was on skis again, for the first time in twelve years. Instantly, I could ski as badly as I did twelve years earlier! The active holiday in Switzerland kept my mind off the prospect of the return visit to hospital. The day came in early January. The doctor called me into the consulting room. 'I think we have some good news.' After looking at the healing wound, he said that the condition had been a very rare non-malignant tumour in the Leydig cells, which they might wish to monitor, because of the rarity of the complaint. 'Go and celebrate the rest of your life.' He seemed as pleased as I was, not least that we had had a good skiing holiday. I wrote to the hospital, to thank them for the great service supplied by the NHS and, in particular, the staff of RUH Bath. It had been excellent and, having worked in the public service all my life, I know how valued is a letter of appreciation.

The entry in my diary read, 'He keeps His word. "You shall not die but live and declare the works of the Lord." There is much more for me to do. God is faithful and can be trusted. All is well.'

With the help of family and friends, I had faced up to my Goliath. It is no use facing your Goliaths until you have gained some experience at bear and lion killing. The bears and lions which may be work, finances or relationships may seem important, but they pale into insignificance, compared with facing the prospect of death. It is going through this experience which makes you aware of what is crucial or trivial. The most vital thing in life is to have a relationship with the only true God who you can come to know as your Heavenly Father. This is one of the things that makes Christianity unique.

Twelve

WORKING WITH UNCERTAINTY

Being self-employed is quite different from receiving a regular monthly salary cheque. With the benefit of personal experience, I now have a great deal more understanding for the self-employed and small entrepreneurs than I had before. The concern is for the next contract. Living without security in employment can be stressful and requires a new attitude. An outplacement package proved invaluable in motivating me to promote myself – not an easy thing to do if you have only been used to applying for jobs and attending interviews.

When I moved from full-time employment to portfolio working, my mentor John Webster, provided by Coutts Career Consultants, had all the skills and knowledge and experience. He challenged and inspired me to do the things I most enjoyed and was best at doing, not least mentoring others. He encouraged me to write down my achievements, skills and experience, focussing clearly on what I wanted to achieve for the future. Hilary took part in the initial sessions, because it is important to share a future vision with your wife. We put together a dynamic CV which even impressed me by its brevity – and I was all set, though a little reluctant, to send it out to my network, and to their network of contacts.

I set out my business plan of what I hoped to achieve and was encouraged to make a list of all the ambitions and desires yet to be fulfilled in my life. This set in train a series of events which I now look back on with some amazement. Not only were financial targets met but, through a whole series of meetings and often unplanned contacts, work filled the diary. 'God created us for work' is a theme on which I often teach at Christian business courses. There were special events like Spring Harvest 'At work together' conferences which led on to speaking on workplace issues at the main event at Minehead over a number of years and being a speaker at the Evangelical Alliance 'Reasons for Hope' conference at Cardiff. One engagement leads to another and the diary was full again with conferences, Church weekends, Stewards Trust Houseparties, and one-night stands. I surprised myself by writing some books, thanks to the encouragement of my publisher. Even more surprising, I became good at selling them.

Prayer, and seeking God's direction, is vitally important, because there is nothing more debilitating than spending hours of time and energy pursuing jobs or contracts you are not going to get. Not all work is paid employment. The quality of life for so many is only sustained by those who give voluntary help. It is also good to give priority to doing things that give you the most satisfaction and enjoyment.

It was during a paid mentoring assignment for a city local authority that the opportunity to become part-time interim Treasurer for a newly created unitary authority arose. There followed a number of contracts to undertake independent reviews, and a further paid mentoring task with another senior local government manager who was leading a politically challenging and sensitive economic development project.

It was sitting next to the Head of Public Sector Consultancy for one of the major accountancy firms at a Christmas Carol Service in Bath Abbey that led to an exciting opportunity to work on a project team advising the Cabinet of the Government of Uzbekistan. It was undertaking a research project for the LGMB that led to my first publication *Making Allowances for Members*, and subsequently working for over 40 councils as advisor/chairman of Independent Panels advising on the very sesitive issue of Member Allowances and expenses. It was through this that other work came to conduct independent reviews, including work with the Audit Commission and The Association of Electoral Administrators. I chaired a very sensitive public enquiry for Gloucester County Council.

My ambitions to become a Company Chairman and non executive Director were fulfilled. I became a non Executive Director of Wiltshire Health Authority and chaired the Audit committee. Comuting to London was required for the post of Interim Director of Finance for the English Tourism Council.

In many situations the opportunity to witness as a Christian was readily available and impacted on people's lives, sometimes with life-changing results.

It is vital to be positive in the time of uncertainty, and always to have hope. Without hope you cannot exercise faith. You establish your hope picture by what you speak – what you declare about the future. When I look back I can see that God has given me the things that I have declared, even what may seem trivial. I often declared that I wanted to be 'best man' ten times – and I have just done my tenth! Often God will give you an indication about some future direction in which He is planning to take you. He does not tell you more than you can handle. If it were otherwise, the danger would be that you try to speed up the process, so messing up the plan. This is the exciting situation we are now in, having been given very direct words about the future. In the end all that matters is fulfilling God's purpose for your life.

Exercising patience can be difficult but it is only with faith and patience that you obtain God's promises. When I first spoke on this subject I asked God for a personal illustration. This was given to me during a winter when we had heavy snow. The skis came down from the loft and we skied down the slopes of the lovely Limpley Stoke Valley, to the home of our great friends Tim and Wendy Wheeldon, for lunch. The valley looked superb. The sunshine and fresh unspoilt snow covered the trees and ground. Smoke curled up from the chimneys as, together with Tim, I looked out on the landscape which years before had encouraged the hymn writer to compose, 'For the beauty of the earth.' Tim understood weather conditions. He had been a helicopter pilot for the Navy and had then flown commercially to oil rigs off the coast of Nigeria. 'Do you know, Don, it always rains or snows heaviest just before it stops,' he said. This was God's answer. In other words, just when you are finding things impossible, this is the time to hold on and not to be panicked into action. God's answer is on the way! No matter how many times we learn this lesson, it does not seem to make it any easier for the next time.

One thing that has become clear to me over the years is the importance of mentoring. Certain individuals have been role models for me, and have been provided especially when I was going through those tough learning experiences of life. They were people who taught me how to turn setbacks into springboards. It was at a lunchtime meeting I organised for business people in Bath that Steve Stanley spoke to me to say that the previous night he had a dream about me, and that it was like Elijah and Elisha. I thought 'Oh – no, I am about to die.' He assured me it was not that, but it was that I had to share my anointing/experience with six other men God would show me, and that as a result my anointing would go to a higher level. So I have tried to mentor and encourage six younger men God has shown me. It is a very rewarding experience to act as a mentor – to see others win and fulfil their potential. How do you gain the credibility to take on the role? – through age, experience, reading, success, being known for honesty and being positive. Mentoring is extremely satisfying when you see the person you are mentoring face the challenge of change, new opportunity or increased responsibility, and grow through the experience.

If you want to know how to mentor from a distinctly Christian perspective I would highly recommend the recently published book by Simon Edwards, *BE – A Disciple's Journey* (published by Releasing Leadership; see pages 146–153).

A part of my work I greatly enjoy is being a motivational speaker, and one of the subjects I often address is 'What will be your legacy from the workplace?' It is good to have your ambitions fulfilled and to develop others to do the same. I hope there are many who would say 'Don Latham helped me to fulfil my potential.' They are part of my legacy from the workplace. Reshaping organisations to become more effective was an important part of my role, and I hope that part of my legacy was encouraging people to give their best and to embrace the future and change with confidence. Identifying future leaders and building effective teams to achieve exceptional results was I hope another part of my legacy. But what inspired me most in the workplace was to see people coming to Christ, for they are part of an eternal legacy. Colleagues who were motivated, encouraged, touched, healed but, more importantly, born again.

Another theme I have spoken about on many occasions is honesty, integrity and truth telling. One of the best attended lectures given in a series at Bath University was not from one of the eminent Christian professors, but given by me. The title was, 'Can you be honest and successful?' They sold more copies of this lecture than of the others. There are major problems facing our society which are economic, social, and political. But I believe the more fundamental problems are moral and spiritual. At the sixth form of Bristol Grammar I gave the same lecture. The sad thing was that I was regarded by some as an 'anachronism'. They thought that success and honesty in the business world were incompatible.

Thirteen

KNOWING AND BEING A FATHER

I am writing this chapter in my study, exactly forty-seven years since our wedding day on August 6th, 1966. Next to our relationship with God, marriage and family life are the most important things in our lives, and the areas most under attack in our society. It has been said that behind every successful man there is a surprised woman. Certainly, I could not have achieved all that has happened in my life without the love, support and understanding of my best friend and wife, Hilary.

One Sunday I was up early, because I was to speak at a church that morning and still not clear about the message. To aid my concentration I did some Vaxing in the lounge. Praising in the Spirit as I worked, I asked God for direction. The thought came clearly. 'I want to set them free from their "if onlys".' That was all I heard from the Lord. When we arrived at the church and joined in the time of praise and worship, nothing more came, until I was called forward to speak by the pastor, the Reverend John Solly, who had given me a very positive introduction. As I walked forward, another thought came strongly to mind: 'Numbers 13:17'. As I invited the congregation to turn to the passage, it was with some interest that I turned to find out what it said, because this was going to be my theme. It was the account of Moses sending out men to spy out the promised land. As you remember, they returned with mixed reports. I read on to 14:2,

'If only we had died in the land of Egypt! Or if only we had died in the wilderness!' (NKJV)

That morning, I prayed for many people to be set free from their 'if onlys'. We all have them. If we do not learn to let go of them, we fail to receive from God the healing, restoration, and movement to new things, that He longs to give us. He is the God of the present and the future. His plans for us are always the best.

My own 'if only' concerned the family. Friends said that I would regret the amount of time I spent at work and on unproductive church activity. They were right. God's priority is our relationship with Him, our marriage and our family. They are strong for us but, when I realised that I should have given them, especially the children, more time, He heard my prayer. Both Peter and Vicky stayed with us at home until they got married – Peter returning to us after university. As I drove to work in my MGBGT, I would speak over them God's favour and that they would be our best friends – and they are. We still go on family holidays together, and we go to good places – including now our three exceptionally talented and fun grandchildren.

With my own struggle to know God as Father, I became very aware of the importance of knowing your own human father, because this is the model we have subconciously adopted in our understanding of God. Because of my own father's work commitments, sickness and early death, I never really knew a father at those critical times of growing up. But God provided other men to mentor me, and also women who could minister into my life and provide good counsel, great example, and godly wisdom. In my teens it was men like Jack Stordy and James Alcock who had been inspirational and encouraging. Then later there was a former missionary called Ruth Webley who gave us such wise advice. It was at a teaching session I was undertaking in Northumberland that Dorothy Vickers had a revelation about my childhood that, with prayer ministry, set me free to understand just how much God loved me.

Paul's letter to the Romans tells believers of the '...Spirit of adoption by whom we cry out, "Abba, Father". (See Romans 8:14–15). 'Abba' is translated 'Daddy', an intimate term. Many Christian believers are now coming into a more intimate relationship with their Heavenly Father. A few weeks before writing this chapter, when praying with the organising team prior to speaking at an event called Box Filling Station, a well-known

Christian had a word for me: 'God says you are His precious boy.' Especially at my age, that is wonderful to know!

My message to men reading this book would be: give priority to your family. Hilary understood the importance of this. She made the choice to take ten years out of her teaching career to give priority time in those early years of the children's lives. We were financially able to do that. Even though it meant going without other things, it has proven to be well worth it. We have seen as a family that God honours those who honour Him.

One evening, Peter was playing cricket for Monkton Combe Junior School. He loves cricket and still plays for a club team today. He opened the batting against a much better team, who had scored an impressive total before declaring in expectation of an early result. He batted through the whole innings. As the pavilion lights became brighter and brighter, the match was drawn to a close. He had saved the day. I was so proud of him, and a little guilty that I had prayed so hard for his success!

Hilary had gone back to teaching. Her job had come in a remarkable way. There was a simple conversation with the heavenly Father, when she had said she would like a local job teaching sixth form Biology, to fit in with the children's schooling. A few weeks later, a coffee morning brought about a contact with the wife of the Head of Monkton Combe. The conversation led to the suggestion that she should contact the Head, who was looking for a part-time Biology teacher for the sixth form. Hilary was appointed, and started teaching there the next term.

During morning break, one Saturday, Hilary felt prompted to pray for Vicky's protection. At the same time, sitting in Bath having coffee and reading the Times, the same thought came to me. Vicky came home at lunchtime with a letter in a sealed envelope. It was from the Head, explaining that the girls had been out on a cross-country run when a strange man had tried to grab Vicky. She had managed to run away and get into school through a back entrance. The police had been called and were interviewing the children.

We were to see God protect us on a number of occasions. Part of the lesson for us was to recognise when God was warning us. It is important to learn the lessons when it is not life threatening. One bank holiday, I had to drive north to speak at an FGBMFI dinner in Chorley. The time I had allowed was not sufficient to provide for any traffic delays, so it was a relief to have negotiated the M5/M6 link in the Midlands. It was near the Stafford junction that the thought came to me: 'Turn on the radio.' The first thing I heard was that there had been a fire at a motorway service station. The M6 was blocked in both directions, with a rapidly growing tail-back of cars. My immediate thought was, 'I will turn off and go via Stoke.'

'Don't go via Stoke,' the radio announcer said. 'There has been a football match and the traffic leaving the ground has added to the congestion.' It was like having a conversation with the BBC – but the source of the guidance was God. I thought, 'OK, I will go via Cheshire to the west of the M6,' and I did, arriving at the meeting in time for dinner. Not listening to God would have prevented me from getting to the meeting. Travelling back, one Saturday morning, from a breakfast in Plymouth, I was almost home. Travelling through the country lanes, I experienced the same inner voice saying, 'If you don't slow down and someone comes round the next corner in the middle of the road at speed, you will be a write-off.' I applied my brakes, and the car coming towards me missed me by inches as I took the next bend!

Doing so much travelling, there are so many stories about car journeys, but the most significant for us as a family happened when were making our first skiing trip together. The early morning drive to Gatwick had been preceded by the task of fitting all our equipment, and the children, into the car. The jigsaw puzzle complete, we set off in excitement down the A36 trunk road to Salisbury. It is well named as a trunk road, because of the way in which it winds down the valley, with high banks and trees on both sides of the road. It was on such a section that a lorry approached us. Suddenly, from behind the lorry, a car appeared at speed, committed to overtaking. The next few moments became like watching a slow motion movie. I pulled hard over to the side, and as the two vehicles – one in our lane – came closer to us, it was obvious there was no room for the manoeuvre. We faced a head-on collision. I found myself calmly putting my hand on the windscreen, saying, 'Jesus protect us.' What happened next theological liberals call 'a temporary suspension of the natural order.' Bible-believers call it a miracle! In the blink of an eye, the car in front of us was now alongside us, and gone. There did not appear to be a gap. We sat there silently, then drove ahead, not speaking for some time. We had all shared an amazing experience of God's protection.

God is interested in the everyday things of our lives. I had to learn that He was ready to intervene, at all times, on our behalf. We were about to return to the Scillies, following a break of many years. This was our favoured location for family holidays, when the children were young. As the helicopter approaches St Mary's, having given you the first view of these low-lying islands, with their white sandy beaches, you are relieved to know things have not changed. A boat ride away from the main islands, are small islands, with deserted beaches. On such a visit we had spent a relaxing day on Bryher when Vicky realised she had lost a gold ring, which had been given her by Hilary's mother, Esther. They had prayed a prayer that the ring would be found by someone honest, and kept for her. Returning to the island a few days later, enquiries were made at the pub about the ring. Amazingly, a man with a metal detector had found the ring and handed it in. On being given a description by Vicky, he returned it to her. Years later, another lost item was a car. Vicky had been working in Bath on a bank holiday, while Hilary and I had been touring West Wiltshire after a picnic lunch at Stourhead. We returned to a crying daughter. Her pride and joy, a Morris Minor car, had been stolen from Pulteney Street. As Hilary consoled and prayed with her, a clear word came to me. 'If you go into Bath, I will show you where it is.' So I told them what I believed God had said. We all drove into Bath, knowing clearly where to find the car. It was, just as we expected, parked at the bottom of a block of flats in Snow Hill! Vicky and Hilary drove to the Police Station to report the car had been found, less than ninety minutes after it had been reported lost.

'We couldn't have done it that quickly,' the bemused constable said. I often wonder what the thief thought when he discovered the car he had stolen had disappeared. When Vicky recounted this to her boyfriend, later that evening, he just stared at me. I hid behind The Times. (It was the broadsheet version at that time). 'Now I know why they used the name Latham on the first Barclaycard adverts,' he said.

We were learning to walk by faith. One day, some hot oil burst into Hilary's face when she was cooking. She rebuked it in the name of Jesus, and suffered no burns. My training on how to pray for healing had begun in the family.

Hilary's mother had had a growth on her arm. Following a visit to the doctor, an operation was planned. It was Christmas, and I knew it was right to pray, but this was all very new to me, and I held back. A few weeks later, after a business trip to Exeter, I called in to see her, and again held back from praying until, having prepared to leave, I suddenly felt a warmth in my hands and blurted out, 'Esther, it is your healing.' Putting my hand round the bandage, I prayed a very simple prayer. A couple of weeks later, at the doctor's surgery, when the bandage was removed, there was no sign of the growth – just skin like a baby's.

At a speaking engagement, the organiser told me she had spoken to my daughter on the telephone. 'She is so proud of you,' she said.

'At last I have arrived as a father,' was my thought. 'Did she say why?' I asked.

'Oh yes, because you have appeared three times in Private Eye.' This was not the answer I expected, but it underlines why I never found pride a problem – because I have family and friends! The children happened to be with us at a well attended FGB dinner in Hull. The excellent and exuberant Chapter President – David Fotherby – made such an enthusiastic anouncement that tapes of my talk would be available at the end of the evening at what I thought was a very modest price. 'Never worth it,' was Vicky's comment in a voice that everyone could hear. It got the best laugh of the evening.

Our heritage is so important. My grandfather seemed at times to be a strange man. He would spend hours reading his Bible and praying. He even understood Leviticus! How he prayed for us, and how I thank God for him now, as well as for my Christian uncles and aunts. Each year we would all make the long trek to Weymouth for a family holiday, and the family photo-album contains the records of this annual excursion. It was good to recount these happy times on a recent trip with my sister. But I am most thankful for my mother who, through her long life and many years as a widow, had a strong, simple faith – a bedrock of my life. The first members of Hilary's family, whom I met only a few weeks after our first date, said, 'Oh good, another accountant in the family.' Hilary's uncle Maurice, whose main loves were cricket and Crusaders, was a great man of prayer. I discovered this on a visit with him to Israel. He knew his Bible so well that places became alive as he related them to the Word of God.

What a privilege to have such an inheritance, and how important to pass it on.

'...And you shall receive the gift of the Holy Spirit. For the promise is to you and to your children, and to all who are afar off, as many as the Lord our God will call'

Acts 2:38b–39, NKJV

The joy of our being from two strong Christian families is that we shall have a reunion in heaven one day. It is a great blessing to have such a godly heritage.

Fourteen

A SECOND CHANCE

I was introducing the main speaker at an FGBMFI West of England Men's Advance at Sidholm in Sidmouth in February 1994. I had never met John Barr before but was told he was well known in London for his prophetic ministry. So I was encouraging the men to listen carefully to what God would say through him. He got up and turned to look at me....

'As you got up, before you said anything, (I've never met you), I felt that God has given you a Joseph spirit. God is going to send you ahead. He is going to bury you for a time. You are going to go under cover because God wants to reveal at a later date. As Joseph went into Egypt for God's people, God is sending you ahead into Egypt in situations, and I believe that God is going to cause you to touch the pillars of our society....'

John was speaking these words to me in front of all these men. This was not the first time this has happened to me when introducing a main speaker. The word continued to flow and he described a time that would feel like being put in silence, a covering, a feeling of being wiped out, of being degraded, with no name, no credibility.' God was saying that it was His problem and not mine and that He would bring me out of that situation and cause me to become a person who would give away all God had given to me.

John got the men to gather round and described how after a time of silence God would use me 'in a very positive and very critical situation in this nation.' At the time I was doing a national job, which I loved, but he went on to describe how I would lose the job – although I did not recognise it at the time. The prophecy was not a comfortable word but all the many witnesses were saying 'Amen'. I knew what they were thinking: 'I am glad that is not going to happen to me.' I thought the speaker was having an off day and I listened to the tape only once, and threw it away. But within twelve months I left the national job with feelings John had described so accurately.

Life continued and other consultancy work came in. Christian ministry opportunities developed in most unexpected ways to more than fill the diary. But by the time my 60th came I was feeling depressed, constantly tired, and that things were coming to an end. Others may not have been aware how I was feeling because I am a good actor and have some ability to make others laugh. One day when I was feeling 'wiped out' I remembered the prophecy given to John Barr and I rang a friend in Cornwall to see if he had kept a copy of the tape. He had, and sent it to me.

How often I have played that tape which described so clearly events that had already taken place, were now happening, and some of which are still to come. An uncomfortable word brings great comfort when you know it is the truth and can recognise that God is in control and 'means it for good'.

Nevertheless, my health was not good and I decided, following discussion with my doctor, to withdraw from speaking engagements for a time – although I did complete some long-standing engagements. It is hard to say that you cannot come in twelve months' time because you are currently not feeling well and this is compounded in your thinking when you have in the past exercised a healing ministry. The short course of medication worked, but the main healing came through a small group of Christian friends who prayed for me and in particular Hilary.

There was no rationale to the way I was thinking and feeling. My symptoms, taken individually, seemed so minor except for a bug I caught which caused a dramatic loss of weight. My first inkling that it could be more serious came at a Public Enquiry in the spring of 2003, which I had been asked to Chair for Gloucester County Council. This was a high profile media event. The case of an elderly women who had been required to move because the residential home had put up their charges.

I was coming down the main staircase of County Hall to meet

the media and had to hold on to the balustrade to retain my balance. This loss of balance got worse over the following months although we went on holidays and endeavoured to live a normal life. That is not easy when you have lived life 110% – to find that you do not have the energy, have frequent nausea, and lose your confidence because your balance has gone. Another visit to the doctor and a thorough check up lined me up, along with other tests, for a scan at Royal United Hospital (RUH) in Bath.

Little did I know that God would pre-empt all this with His own precise timetable. I was feeling so down I had been listening to all the negatives that Satan could throw at me. I actually said to Hilary over breakfast one day, 'I feel the whole of my life has been wasted.' Within thirty minutes the front door bell rang and there was Prof. Roy Peacock, a great friend and near neighbour. He describes the incident in his prayer letter as follows:

Recently, the Lord gave me a word for a person I know well to say 'Nothing has been wasted.' By way of confirmation, I was drawn to the story of the feeding of the five thousand where Jesus exhorts his disciples to gather up the fragments 'that nothing be lost.' Why was the word 'wasted' used rather than 'lost' I wondered but held on to it. Cautious about knocking on doors to prophesy, it was three weeks later that I knew the prompting to go to this friend. I gave him the word and, after some thought, he said, 'I was having breakfast with my wife an hour ago and said, "I feel that the whole of my life has been wasted."'

Like Job you can speak such rubbish when you are depressed. Remember, he declared that God gives and takes away. It took a wise young man called Elihu to put him straight. 'Job speaks without knowledge, his words are without insight,' he says.

I have seen God do such great things and have witnessed the blind receiving their sight, the deaf hearing, the mute speaking and the cripple walking. I have known God's supernatural protection and direction, but most important of all the work of the Spirit to help lead many into the Kingdom, including a number of colleagues at work. The experience over the next few weeks was to bring about a complete change in my understanding and actions.

Having not felt well for about two years, I had been booked by the doctor to have a scan. Things got accelerated when I had a fall at home on 21st February, a Saturday evening. As I had been unconscious briefly, Hilary called the ambulance and I was taken to RUH Bath.

The ambulance crew arrived from Trowbridge in ten minutes and were brilliant in insisting that I needed to go to A & E. Vicky, our daughter, came to the hospital to be with us and to take Hilary home. The doctors and nurses there were excellent. I was in two nights before the results of a scan revealed that I had an Acoustic Neuroma, and I was transferred to Frenchay as an emergency admission on 24th February. God looked after every detail. The scanner had broken down at Frenchay and I could be dealt with immediately because the machine at RUH was working. Peter our son had driven from Cardiff and was waiting to welcome me to Frenchay and was so positive about what had happened – that it was going to be sorted.

The consultant at Bath was most encouraging. The good news was that these tumours tend to be benign, which is what it proved to be, but it was large and had been growing slowly, probably over many years. They started, even before I left Bath, to give me steroids to prepare for a major operation. On 1st March I had an eight-hour operation and the tumour was removed without any damage to nerves, etc. God had given me three Christian nurses on three wards and the best team, led by Mr Nelson, for a day in the operating theatre. The truth is I had no fear or concerns about the process and could not wait to get it done. The doctors, nurses and other staff were brilliant. One of the many good things about the crisis was that it has brought our family closer than we have ever been, and this has certainly re-ordered my priorities for the future. After God now comes family, not just in theory but in practice.

I had gradually lost the hearing in my left ear following the manifestation of tinnitus on a ministry trip to Argentina in 1999. I had accepted this as part of the ageing process. But in tests done prior to the operation it was to be confirmed that I would never hear again with my left ear. It could only be restored if I received a miracle, which I am believing will happen soon. I told the Consultant that hundreds of people would be praying for him and he welcomed any support. It was true that the Christian network was so effective that people were praying in Argentina, India, Australia, Israel, and throughout the UK. I did not want people to be bothered with my problems but God thought differently and I have never felt so supported and loved in my life. I get quite emotional when I think and talk about it.

The initial recovery was not pleasant but was as expected by the doctors and as the anaesthetist had warned me. All the staff were so understanding and I would later miss the routine you get into in life in hospital. The staff were, without exception, caring and highly professional in all they did. You leave a hospital full of admiration for those in the caring professions. The timing through the whole process was perfect. I came home from hospital on 10th March. Hilary dropped me at the front door and drove round the back of the house to park the car. Thanks to my loss of weight, which people say has made me look better than for years, my trousers fell round my ankles. It was late in the evening and fortunately was not seen by neighbours. I cannot speak too highly of the NHS but it was good to be home.

Most significantly I came to know God in a new way as a loving heavenly Father whose timing is perfect and who loves me for who I am not what I do for Him. As a result I started to hear Him speak to me so clearly, and as I was obedient to do what He told me to do then the next instruction came. Interestingly, it started with work and He told me the things I should do and those from which I should resign. As soon as I had taken action He moved on to Christian activity and had me resign from all my Trusteeships and Management Boards. One action I struggled with was to shred my old sermon notes! They were a comfort to me. It was always good to know I had 300+ sermons/talks to fall back on. But I did it and felt a sense of release as they went in the bin or through the shredder. When this was done we moved on to practical things associated with our house and finances.

It was not all over but simply the clearing of the decks so that so many unfulfilled dreams and desires could be realised. It was truly like experiencing a second chance at life. He told me that He would now give me fresh revelation, and the future priority for my teaching had to be the Kingdom of God.

Fifteen

CHRISTIAN RETIREMENT

I actually thought that as retirement beckoned I could not do more but I could do fewer things better, with more time to prepare fresh material for talks and more time for writing and watercolour painting. But there was and is to be no retirement plan. Retirement is not featured or mentioned in the Bible. Often it was in people's latter years that the greatest things were accomplished. For many today the move from paid work to voluntary work releases them to a whole new range of opportunity of service in the local community (the big community) and internationally.

To be a success it is important to know your strengths and weaknesses. It was at a major Spring Harvest event that I met a dynamic and very successful businesswoman/mentor who at the time was a managing director. Having heard my presentation, she very helpfully suggested that I would benefit from undertaking a leadership interview. It was rigorous, and her assessment of me as a leader accurate, sensitive and challenging. I have tried to address the weaknesses like the tendency to over commit, the need to delegate and to keep my natural competitiveness under control. But on the strength side my desire to see others grow and develop did come through. She said that making the most of your strengths and working with these was the key to finding the greatest fulfilment and opportunities to fulfil my life purposes. And she was right.

During the years since I was baptised in the Spirit, many things have happened which are beyond the scope of normal coincidence and accident, confirming to me without question both that there is a God, and that I have come to know Him, through His Son Jesus Christ. You might propose other explanations for my experience, but one thing it is difficult to explain away is the accuracy of revelation gifts of the Spirit such as prophecy. We have a small group of people who pray for us, sometimes every day as was the case with Pastor Janet Woods from Warminster, who did this every day when I was CEO in West Wiltshire. She had a remarkable role in confirming God's direction for my life by quoting His Word to me. This often came in an early morning call when, 'Good morning, Don' would be the introduction to the latest pearl of wisdom. Everything has to be tested but the timing and accuracy of the 'words' we have received over the years has often been quite remarkable.

We have had words expressing God's total generosity, spiritual abundance, and victory; and that we would have a ministry to the very poor and the very rich. So not surprisingly one of the most significant things we have done in our lives is to be part of an exciting work in Andhra Pradesh in India which we visit each year. Some of our best friends, and those we most admire, are in India. We have also developed friendships with people who enjoy the best of material things, many of whom we have met when we travel. How we have particularly enjoyed return trips to Australia, New Zealand , USA and the West Indies to spend time with them. They are very special people.

When God speaks it is so important to listen, then take action. It was in April 1981 that God spoke to me when I was in the bath. Hilary called from the bedroom.

'This is God's word for you – from Titus 1:1–3,' she said.

'... I have been sent to bring faith to those God has chosen and to teach them to know God's truth – the kind of truth that changes lives – so that they can have eternal life, which God promised them before the world began – and he cannot lie. And now in his own good time he has revealed this good news and permits me to tell it to everyone. By command of God our Saviour, I have been trusted to do this work for him.' (TLB)

After this, new opportunities opened up all over the UK and overseas in quite an amazing way. One such night was in Farnham. It was a very smart hotel, speaking to a group of about fifty business people. One man appeared to be taking notes, which is not usual.

At the end of the evening he tore out a page of his pad, giving it to me as he left. I stuffed it in a pocket and read it the next day.

'My son , be prepared for a major change in your circumstances. You have been a good and faithful servant to me, and I delight to reward you so, as the chances come , lean on me and come more and more into my presence. I will not leave you or forsake you. I will bless you and support you. This is my desire for you, that you will move as I lead, and follow my will without question.'

This was just a few months before the move to West Wiltshire District Council, to be Chief Executive. By this time I was ready for a move, and just waiting for the opportunity. The Farnham evening was memorable, for another reason. A director of one of our top electronics companies was there with his wife, who was crippled with arthritis. We prayed, and saw no immediate change. The next morning she was in the bathroom and realised she had got there without her walking aids. She had been completely healed.

It was good that we had such clear words about the move to West Wiltshire. There were a number of confirmations from mature Christians, which gave assurance when problems emerged. If you know that God has put you in a place, it does not make it easy but it does give you confidence. When the problems became public, letters of support came from all round the country. There was support in the House of Commons, when a number of Early Day Motions were raised. People had been praying even before it became public news. As the letters literally poured in, and the telephone rang continuously, there was one predominant word.

'No weapon formed against you shall prosper, and every tongue which rises against you in judgment you shall condemn. This is the heritage of the servants of the Lord, and their righteousness is from Me, says the Lord'

Isaiah 54:17 (NKJV)

Over the years, people had visions of me in radio and television studios, and working with press. I could have no idea that a move to a quiet District Council was to make those things reality. When I knew it was time to leave this post I asked for a third confirmation, whilst sitting at my desk early in the morning. 'Good morning Don! The answer to your question is positive,' Janet said. 'Promotion', and she followed it with words of encouragement which were so specific for the next position.

I had retired from being a Director of FGBMFI when someone refered to me as an FGB dinosaur! So I was very reluctant when I was being pushed to start a new event for men in Bath by two men: a young man I was mentoring – he was very fit and a keen boxer – and an accountant whom God told to fund the first three events. My church home group leader, knowing nothing of the way I was being directed, had a vision of me launching a shiny new fishing boat, and after launching many other new boats followed. I was still holding back, and God said to me, 'If you do not do it now – you are being disobedient.'

Simple market research revealed that the best time to get men together was for a Saturday breakfast. Many churches run successful fellowship style Saturday breakfasts but I wanted to arrange a 'cringe free' event that any man would feel comfortable and confident to invite a neighbour, work colleague or friend to attend, that would be inspiring, enjoyable, and potentially life changing. It would be designed to attract men who would not initially attend a church-based breakfast and a key word for the event would be excellence.

I set out the concept in a 'discussion paper' for consideration by church leaders and they responded that 'we are positive regarding your ideas for men, so feel free to proceed with our blessing and support.'

What you name a thing is important and the young men I approached to be part of this new venture did not like a title including the word 'businessman'. They were engineers, teachers, computer specialists, solicitors, operational managers, etc. They also did not want to join a 'fellowship', and being busy men with their families, careers, and churches, only wanted to be part of an activity requiring a minimum time commitment. I did not know what to do about the name but was clear in my mind that Graham Dacre, an old friend and Christian businessman from Norwich, should be our first speaker. He duly agreed to come and it was from him the name MENUNITED came. His wife had thought of this name for a recent men's dinner organised by their own church that had attracted over 200 men. So with their permission the name was adopted and has been very well received. It is simple, 'blokish' and not stuffy.

MENUNITED, www.menunited.info, is a men only ministry/ event. Men from all Christian denominations, and especially non Christians, are welcome to attend. Unity is a key to seeing spiritual growth and an outpouring of the Holy Spirit (Psalm133) and we have seen the evidence of this since we started in May 2008. This is an event not suitable for church premises or the back room of a poor quality hotel. A smart restaurant or bar is ideal .

At a prayer meeting for evangelism in the City of Bath in September 2008, a word was given for MENUNITED, from Micah: 'I will surely gather all of you.... I will set them together like sheep in a fold, like a flock in its pasture, a noisy multitude of men' (4:12). Men have travelled from surrounding towns and villages. Others have come much greater distances and all like what they see and experience.

I have been very careful about taking on new commitments but so many things are happening in Bath and it is good to be part of the Healing on the Streets (HOTS) team praying for people outside the Abbey. To be a Trustee of the excellent World Sport Ministries and to financially support Genesis and other organisations like Street Pastors, Food bank, and Youth for Christ, where Christians are working together to meet the needs of the most vulnerable in our community. We get great pleasure from being on the teaching team of Embassy Bible College. There is united prayer for the city in the Abbey twice a year, and a real desire to see the Kingdom of God expressed in every part of city life, and through celebrations like 'Love Bath', our annual party in the park to bring Christians together and to bless our city. This is the same place that I declared in 1963: ' Father, this is the place I would love to live and serve you.'

One of the most exciting recent developments is the work of The Filling Station Trust (www.thefillingstation.org.uk), where I am a Trustee and recommended speaker. A work that started locally is now rapidly spreading throughout the UK and to other countries. It is not a new independent church movement, rather a model of how existing churches can work together to bring new spiritual life to their areas and in the process bring many new people to faith in Jesus Christ. We want to see Christian communities grow and become healthier in their local expression. Mid-week meetings are designed to be overtly spiritual, but presented in a manner that those outside the existing church would feel comfortable in experiencing. Meetings are usually held on a monthly basis and aim to be short, sharp and focussed in character. They are a place to network and make new friendships, but more importantly a place to build faith and meet God.

We did say to God that we would go anywhere for Him as long as we did not have to leave our doctors' practice. But we love travel and have visited more than fifty countries and ministered in more than half of them. We have made one house move and yet have not had to leave our doctors' practice! Life has always been full and at times too hectic. We did eventually have a proper sabbatical in Australia and New Zealand. Ten weeks visiting great friends and travelling through some of the best countryside in the world. We came back with a completely different perspective on how we should be living and the desire to spend less time at meetings. It was for us truly life changing and in particular about how we should spend our time in future. This was compounded by many books given to us to read following our return. We now see doing church in quite a new way, and in a way that would increasingly result in faith in action for every church member, not simply a paid team.

There was another remarkable story. I was speaking at a weekend at the united Free Church in Totnes. This had been one of my favourite audit locations when I had worked for Devon County Council. One man came to the evening service, brought by his daughter, who had met some Christians at her university. She wanted to know more. His wife had dressed him and put on his shoes, as usual. He had been in agony for most of the previous eighteen months, suffering from severe back and kidney problems. He shuffled slowly and painfully to the church meeting. A non-Christian, he did not pray for himself, nor did anyone else. Four hours later, he ran home – uphill! He had been completely healed, just sitting there in about the fifth row. His story made a dramatic impact on his family and colleagues at the District Council office. All were invited to hear his remarkable testimony, and to watch his baptism in the river, a few months later.

We experienced a cameo of what we believe is coming when

speaking at a conference in Brunel Manor in April 2009. Someone had a word that Jesus wanted to 'walk amongst his people'. So when I had finished speaking I invited him to walk amongst us. Within a few moments a friend got out of her wheelchair, touched her toes and was completely healed. She got home and had the all clear from her GP, returned her disabled driver badge and cancelled her carers and disability benefits. She left her mobility scooter at Brunel for the benefit of other guests and returned her wheelchair to to the hospital, much to their surprise. In the glory of God's presence you experience the supernatural. That is the realm we expect to operate in this next phase of life.

I still do any work that comes my way and still apply for suitable appointments. Work is my calling, and whilst I am determined to pace myself, retirement is not on the agenda. I am still competing for the best prize and believe the best is yet to come.

On a recent holiday break in Bermuda, God made clear that the biggest things that I have declared in my life are about to happen so we are getting prepared with a great sense of excitement and anticipation. We have had amazing recent confirmations that we are on the edge of a major breakthrough of blessing as we seek to know and to walk in the glory of God. God gave me an action list of things to do and, as I write, I am conscious that rewriting this book is one of things that had to be done – hence the urgency!

Being a Christian does not stop you from making mistakes, as my life shows. God even uses them. There are things we do not understand, and may never understand this side of heaven. Are there some things I can't explain? Yes. But do I have any doubts about my faith? The answer is no. I have a faith that works.

23921730R10064

Made in the USA
Charleston, SC
09 November 2013